# Empty Cradle
# Broken Heart

# *Empty Cradle Broken Heart*

## Surviving the Death of Your Baby

Deborah L. Davis, Ph.D.

FULCRUM PUBLISHING
Golden, Colorado

Library of Congress Cataloging-in-Publication Data

Davis, Deborah L., 1955–
    Empty cradle, broken heart : surviving the death of your baby /
Deborah L. Davis.
              p.        cm.
    Includes bibliographical references and index.
    ISBN 1-55591-063-7 (trade paper)
    1. Perinatal death—Psychological aspects. 2. Bereavement—
Psychological aspects. 3. Adjustment (Psychology) 4. Parent and
child. I. Title.
RG631.D38 1990
155.9'37—dc20                         90-42662
                                               CIP

Printed in the United States of America

0   9   8   7   6   5   4   3   2   1

Fulcrum Publishing
350 Indiana Street
Golden, CO 80401

To all of your babies, loved and remembered still

# Contents

# Preface

One purpose of this book is to let bereaved parents know that they are not alone in their grief. Many mothers and fathers are quoted in this book, and although everyone's grief is unique, the sentiments expressed are common among bereaved parents.

Many parents have experienced the death of a baby—at any time during pregnancy, during delivery, shortly after birth or during infancy. In spite of medical advances, more than one-fourth of all women will at some time experience miscarriage, stillbirth or infant death. Each year in the United States, out of an estimated 4.4 million *confirmed* pregnancies, there are more than half a million miscarriages, twenty-nine thousand stillbirths and thirty-nine thousand infant deaths under 1 year of age. (Some fertility specialists estimate that another one million unconfirmed pregnancies end in miscarriage shortly after embryo implantation, but before the pregnancy is acknowledged.) However, many parents keep their losses and feelings about them a secret, partly because of society's hushed attitudes toward death and partly because many people do not recognize the depth of such losses.

This book strives to cover many different kinds of loss. In ectopic pregnancy, the fertilized ovum becomes lodged outside the uterus, most commonly in the fallopian tube. Surgery is necessary to remove the embryo to save the mother's life. Moreover, if scarring occurs or if a fallopian tube or ovary is removed, the woman's fertility can decrease. First trimester miscarriages often occur for undetectable reasons, and many mothers feel betrayed by their bodies. Many times early miscarriage is treated as a blessing, "nature's way of weeding out the weak." The depth of the loss depends on what meaning the pregnancy held for the parents, but for many, miscarriage is a baby who died. Even during the second trimester when a baby is born too early for any chance of survival, the mother is occasionally not allowed to see the baby, for fear that it will upset her. But for the mother to see her baby is to validate that the child existed and lived inside her.

Some mothers must consent to a therapeutic abortion due to illness, infection, toxemia or other conditions in which pregnancy endangers the mother's life. Other mothers consent because the baby has birth defects. For these mothers, the heartache of making such a decision often goes unrecognized.

During the last trimester, a baby's chances for survival increase with each additional week—up to full term—spent in the womb. However, many premature babies die during delivery or shortly after birth due to immaturity or illness. Sometimes labor is induced when ultrasound tests confirm there is no fetal heartbeat. The mother is then faced with enduring labor and delivery, knowing her baby is already dead. For many stillborn babies, death is caused by umbilical cord constriction, placental abruption, infection or birth defects, but for one-third of stillbirths, the cause of death remains a mystery.

By 38 weeks a fetus is considered to be full term, yet these babies may still die before or during delivery. Even after a baby is born and seems fine, infection may be discovered or may set in, or birth defects incompatible with life outside the womb may be discovered. For some of these babies death comes quickly, while for others death may come only after months of struggle. Some parents face the agonizing decision of whether to attempt treatment or whether to stop it.

According to the National SIDS Foundation, sudden infant death syndrome (the unexpected death of an otherwise healthy baby) is the leading cause of death of babies between 1 month and 1 year of age. The cause or prevention remains a mystery. Thousands more babies succumb to other diseases, infections and accidents every year. For SIDS babies and many babies who contract bacterial or viral infections, death is so swift that the joy of a healthy baby turns to tragedy in a matter of hours. For babies with lingering illnesses, parents feel the additional devastation of watching their suffering or debilitation. For babies who die from accidents such as drowning or automobile collisions, parents may be especially wracked with "what ifs" and "if onlys."

Although babies die for many different reasons, parents share in common a shattering grief. This book is for them.

## ABOUT THIS BOOK

This book doesn't try to tell you how you should feel or what you must do. Rather, it strives to show you the wide range of experiences that can follow the death of a baby and to offer strategies for coping with this loss. With factual information and the words and insights of other bereaved parents, you can establish realistic expectations for your grief. You can also gain reassurance that you are not crazy, you are not the only one who has felt betrayed or angry, you are not the only one to cradle pillows in your empty arms. This book is meant to help you through your grief by giving you things to think about, providing suggestions for coping and encouraging you to do what *you* need to survive your baby's death. Whether your baby died recently or long ago, this information can be useful to you.

It is not necessary to read this book from start to finish. Some sections may feel more appropriate than others at different times, depending on your unique situation, your personality and where you are in your grief. Take in whatever seems helpful, and pass by whatever isn't. Come back to the passages that are particularly comforting, and try reading other parts later.

If reading this book moves you to cry, try to accept this reaction. These are healing tears—of grief and empathy, even joy. They are also tears of courage, health and strength that merge with those of other grieving parents. You are not alone.

# Acknowledgments

This book is based on more than six years of research and clinical work with bereaved parents. The original research for my Ph.D. dissertation was funded in part by the March of Dimes Greater Colorado Chapter and supervised by Robert J. Harmon, M.D., and Marguerite Stewart, R.N., Psy. D., at the University of Colorado Health Sciences Center in Denver. I am indebted to them for guiding me to this important issue: to Bob for taking me on as a graduate student researcher and widening my horizons, and to Margy for opening doors and teaching me so much. I am indebted to Marvin Daehler, Ph.D., and Edward Tronick, Ph.D., my advisers at the University of Massachusetts, for being flexible and having faith in my ability to pull off this daring idea of going to Colorado to finish my graduate work.

Special gratitude also goes to the following women for their support—my co-facilitators at the Boulder County Hospice Pregnancy/Infant Loss Support Group: Jane Karyl, Dee Paddock and Lynn Kimball, R.N., who also helped me compile medical information on physical recovery; my dear friend, Terri Macey, Ph.D., for introducing me to the Pregnancy/Infant Loss Support Group and mostly for all her encouragement and confidence that this book could happen; my editor, Karen Groves, who knew that this book was important and should be published. All five of these women also know firsthand what it is like to have a baby die, and their special sensitivity has influenced my writing.

I am indebted to the mothers who participated in my dissertation research study, for sharing a very personal and painful part of their lives with me. I also want to thank the many parents of the Boulder County Hospice Pregnancy/Infant Loss Support Group, for sharing their stories, struggles and acquired wisdom. Although many names have been changed to ensure anonymity, I hope these mothers and fathers will know how vitally their experiences and insights have contributed to this book.

Bereaved parents are special. They are survivors, and I am always inspired by the courage with which they face their pain, and the strength by which they cope with their devastating loss.

Finally, I am grateful to my husband Ken Kirkpatrick, who has supported and encouraged my desire to write.

# A Parent's Lonely Grief

## THE "D" WORD

In our society, unfortunately, death is not talked about freely. Rather than being seen as an inevitable and natural part of the cycle of life, death has become something we try to avoid. We want to prevent it from happening to us or loved ones. With the discovery of antibiotics and vaccines, we expect our children to survive into adulthood and to outlive us, and most of us expect to live until we are very, very old. With new advances in medical science and technology, many previously fatal conditions are now curable, and it is possible to prolong life almost indefinitely, sometimes without regard to quality of life.

We also avoid contact with the dying and the dead. Up until the middle part of this century, most people died at home. Family members bathed and dressed the body, and friends and relations gathered to view the body and grieve together. Now, most people die in hospitals or nursing homes, and the body is shipped off to be cremated or embalmed according to community health standards. Death has been taken away from the home and family and placed in modern, sterile institutions. Additionally, with increased mobility of families and friends, being present at the death of a loved one, or even attending the funeral, is less likely. These trends make death less familiar to us, and having little experience with dying or death we feel uncomfortable or afraid. Death has been separated from the continuity of life and the living.

We also avoid talking about death. We have all kinds of euphemisms in our language for referring to death, such as: the delicate "passed away," the vague "is no more" or "has been taken," the spiritual "met her maker" or "departed this life," the technical "expired" or "deceased," or the crude "croaked" or "kicked the bucket." Many parents have difficulty talking about death with their children, not wanting to scare them or tarnish their innocence. These attitudes toward death isolate the bereaved, as it is considered almost impolite to talk about the death of a loved one, except at a funeral.

The death of a baby is even more hidden because it violates our expectations. In addition, when we hear about the death of a baby, many of us do not recognize the depth of the loss to the parents. The fact that the baby was in the womb or in the parents' arms for such a brief time adds to their pain and isolation.

## A VIOLATION OF EXPECTATIONS

I was so excited. This was going to be the neatest thing in my whole life. I figured everything was going to go great because you always assume that with your first child. I had a beautiful pregnancy. You couldn't have asked for a nicer one. No morning sickness, I stayed active, it was great.

—Lena

Nowadays, with the development of modern medical procedures and technology, many infertile couples can conceive. Hormonal treatments enable some mothers to maintain a pregnancy through the first trimester. Progress in pregnancy management can increase the chances that a mother will carry a healthy baby to term. Babies born prematurely, who several decades ago would have perished at birth, can now survive infancy. Babies with life-threatening illnesses or birth defects can undergo treatments and surgery, allowing more of them to lead normal lives. Babies can be protected from disease with vaccines, and health can be restored with antibiotics and other medicines.

Expectant parents, having faith in modern medicine and little exposure to infant death, are not likely to seriously consider the possibility that their baby may die, particularly after the first trimester of pregnancy. They naturally assume that a healthy baby will be born, and if sick, that the baby will survive. This assumption accompanies the belief that by "doing all the right things" during pregnancy, even in preparation for pregnancy and certainly after delivery, a healthy baby will be guaranteed.

Medicine isn't what it's cracked up to be. It makes me
realize that medicine and doctors don't hold special
powers. They're as human as the rest of us, and they're
only as good as the job they do. There's just no magic in
medicine, and I think at one time I thought that.

—Kara

I went off the pill for a year and a half in anticipation
because I knew that was something to think about. I did
not drink any caffeine, I did not drink any alcohol, I did
not smoke, I did not do anything. I led my life so perfectly
as far as going by the rules. ... I really wasn't aware that
babies could die. I remember feeling so serene the week
before the baby's birth. I didn't have any worries. I
thought when you made it past a certain point. ...

—Bryn

Everybody thinks of pregnancy as a positive outcome ...
and then to have two miscarriages on top of a stillbirth.
After the second miscarriage, it was, like, this is just
ridiculous, and what am I doing to deserve this. ... I
remember meeting the mother of a test-tube baby and
thinking, "They can do this but they can't take my seven-
and-a-half-pound healthy girl and get her out safely"—
now come on! There's something not right here!

—Holly

Now, when I hear people talk about statistics with
different situations I get a little upset because, you know,
statistics are fine until you become one of them, and then
they take on a different meaning!

—Sarah

With the availability of effective methods of birth control and the
movement of women beyond the realm of homemaking and child
rearing, parents are increasingly likely to plan when and how many
children to have. In addition to the assumption that they will have a
healthy baby, they have an enormous emotional investment in
conceiving within a few months, each pregnancy having a positive
outcome and each child surviving infancy.

When a pregnancy ends in miscarriage or stillbirth, or when a baby dies in infancy, the parents' expectations are cruelly violated, their emotional commitment dashed. Unfortunately, even when they "do all the right things," bad things can happen. To add to the tragedy, bereaved parents often find themselves isolated, as those around them are unable to grasp the full meaning of the loss.

## THE DEPTH OF YOUR LOSS

Miscarriage, stillbirth or the death of an infant is a profound loss because your attachment to the baby can begin even before conception. Even if the pregnancy is unplanned, a special bond materializes as you think about the reality of parenthood.

Throughout this bonding process, you fantasize about the future. You may wonder about your baby's familial characteristics and envision summertimes, wintertimes, holidays, birthdays, graduations, weddings, grandchildren. You look forward to the special "firsts" of childhood, such as baby's first smile, first wobbly steps, first words, first day of school, first school dance. You imagine sharing all kinds of special experiences with your child. In such heartfelt and intimate ways, you become bonded to your baby long before the birth.

When your baby dies, you never get the chance to know the baby in the way that we normally think of knowing someone. But your hopes and dreams for this child have already become a part of your life. You have not only lost a child, you have lost the chance to see your baby grow, become a vital part of the family and realize his or her potential. Your baby's death represents a deeply felt loss of a wished-for child, as well as a loss of your fantasies, hopes and dreams. Indeed, it represents a denial of part of your future, part of yourself.

## SPECIAL DIFFICULTIES

Grieving for a baby is very different from grieving for a spouse, parent, sibling, older child or other loved one. There are many factors that can affect the course of a person's grief, but for a number of reasons, a baby's death is especially difficult to endure.

A baby's death upsets the natural order of life. Many parents are struck with the realization that their children are not supposed to die before they do. It feels so unfair that children, especially babies, can die before they have a chance to grow old and live a full life.

Other parents feel that this experience challenges the way they view life, nature or the universe. Their beliefs are shaken to the core and it can take years to come to terms with the senselessness of their baby's death. Moreover, parents are faced with the difficulty of feeling intensely angry and having no one to hold accountable.

Coping with a baby's death is particularly difficult because the length of time spent with the infant is so brief. When you never or barely get to know your baby outside the womb, you may feel cheated of the chance to learn about this child's special qualities and how he or she would have graced your life.

## FEELINGS OF RESPONSIBILITY

When a baby dies, parents may feel especially responsible for what happened. Grief can be complicated by how long they had been trying to conceive, difficulties during pregnancy or delivery, birth defects, prognosis for future pregnancy, and whether or not they already have healthy children. Mothers tend to feel principally responsible. They may feel like failures as women, angry at their bodies' betrayal or tremendously guilty about what they did or did not do that might have contributed to their babies' death. Many mothers feel angry toward women who seem to renounce the rules of good health and good habits during pregnancy, yet have the satisfaction of healthy babies. All of these normal feelings originate from the belief that they should be able to prevent or avoid such tragedies with "good" behavior.

## LOSS OF THE IDEALIZED BABY

Because you had very little time to get to know your baby, you may have difficulty separating the typical idealized fantasies about this baby from the probable realities. We all fantasize about giving birth to a baby who will grow to attain intelligence, creativity, social skills, beauty, grace, honesty and courage. The reality is that we will probably give birth to a normal child, capable of keeping us up all night, being a picky eater and refusing piano lessons. However, if you did not have the opportunity to know your baby and his or her unique personality, charms and annoyances, it is more difficult to let go of this "perfect" child who never moderated your dreams.

Some of the fantasies you have are not true. You picture
yourself in the spring out there and the baby toddling
around and you're digging in the garden. But that doesn't
happen because you've got to watch that kid every
second. After I had another baby, it helped to see that
reality, and I could finally let go of a lot of those fantasies.

—Bryn

### LOSS OF A PART OF YOURSELF AND YOUR FUTURE

Because fantasies about your baby often reflect personal attributes or
desires, a baby's death may magnify a sense that you have lost a part
of your inner self. Likewise, if you and your baby shared similar
qualities, you may feel like a part of you is missing. Claudia had a
strong kinship with her baby and feels this loss keenly. She says,
"Jacob was such a strong, independent little guy. I felt like I could
have really understood him because he would have been so much like
me, like I would've been able to understand his rebelliousness,
especially as a teenager."

This loss of self is often particularly acute for mothers, as the life
growing inside was physically and psychologically a part of her.

While the death of a parent or friend represents a loss of your
past, when your baby dies you lose a part of your future. You grieve
not only for your baby, but for your parenthood. Times you had
looked forward to—maternity leave, family gatherings and holidays—
can seem worthless or trivial without your baby. If you preferred to
have all your children by a specific age or spaced a certain number of
years apart, the death of your baby means that your family will not
be what you planned. Indirectly, this death represents a missing
branch of the family tree as you consider the prospective generations
that might have been. All of these deficits in your future make it
particularly painful to get on with your life.

I didn't get to take him fishing, and he didn't get to take
swimming lessons, he didn't get to throw rocks in the
pond and make snowballs or have a frog collection. I
would've let him have one too. I was made to be the
mother of a little boy.

—Lena

I had never experienced anything so deadening. You
know the commercial about "celebrate the moments of
your life." I was picturing that—all the family being there
for holidays and other occasions. I pictured us as a family
with the baby sitting around watching the World Series.
All those experiences were so hard to bear. They were
losses each time.

—Bryn

## LACK OF MEMORIES AND RITUALS OF MOURNING

Memories are important for the bereaved. Dwelling on memories is a
way to experience a more gradual goodbye. Unfortunately, when your
baby dies before or shortly after birth, you have only a few memories and
it is unclear how this baby fit into your life. Your baby is gone, and you
have little tangible evidence that he or she really existed.

Grieving is made more painful and complex when the "hello-
goodbye" is so abrupt. Many mothers speak of the shock of experiencing a glowing pregnancy, an uncomplicated delivery or even the return
home of a healthy baby, only to have something go wrong with no
warning. Suddenly their baby is gone. To them, the brief hours or few
months with the baby are not enough time to gather precious memories.

Spending time with the body, arranging a funeral, attending the
burial and recognizing a mourning period are rituals designed to
support the bereaved, but these rituals are often denied, overlooked
or minimized when a baby dies. Rose remembers the limousine driver
on the way to the gravesite making little jokes and chatting about
local and national news events. To her, it summed up the feeling that
her life had frozen and the whole world was going on without her;
that her baby's death was but a droplet of mist that made no ripples
when it hit the water.

## LACK OF SOCIAL SUPPORT

Unfortunately, many friends and relatives do not recognize the depth
of your loss. It is difficult for them to imagine your grief over a baby
you never saw or perhaps held only briefly. Even if your baby died
later in infancy, you may feel as though you are expected to grieve
minimally and be "back to normal" after the first few weeks or
months have passed. Add to this the fact that death is an uncomfortable
topic to discuss, and you may begin to feel isolated, unwelcome to

talk and share your feelings. Because your grief is ignored or considered unnatural, you may wonder if your baby and the events surrounding his or her life and death are insignificant. Moreover, friends and relatives may have never seen the baby, so you have even fewer memories to share with others. These feelings of isolation, being the only one who knew the baby or the only one who cares, can make grieving very painful.

> If my mom died, or my sister, or anybody that had lived for years and years, I would talk about them every now and then. But because my baby wasn't born alive, people think I'm harping on it if I talk about it, which isn't true, not to me.
>
> —Cindy

> It's been four years and I haven't closed the book on it. She was still a part of my life. She was a daughter just like my other daughters are now. I don't think anybody would expect me to forget if Lori or Anna were to die now. I don't think they would force me to get over it, because they're not a newborn, like newborns are something less.
>
> —Rose

> I think it's hard because I think I'm the only one that's thinking about her, and maybe my husband and I wonder if anyone else is thinking about her.
>
> —Kitty

## LACK OF PROFESSIONAL SUPPORT

For parents who have experienced miscarriage, stillbirth or death of an infant, grieving is necessary and healthy. However, it has only been in the last decade or so that health professionals have begun to recognize that these parents *need* to grieve. In the past, it was assumed that parents would not grieve the loss because, after all, "They never really had a chance to know their baby." Parents were admonished for feeling upset or sad, because these feelings were considered destructive and unhealthy, evidence that the parents were "dwelling on the baby" or "crying over spilt milk." Parents were pressured to forget about the baby and to think about having another one. They were dissuaded from cradling their dying baby, for fear that they might have to endure more painful memories. After death, the baby was whisked away to spare the parents the sight of their child and the grief they might have experienced if they had been allowed to hold the baby.

As a result of these attitudes, parents were deprived of expressing love to their baby in physical ways, and they buried their feelings or felt crazy for having them. When friends and family echoed these attitudes, bereaved parents were left with little or no support for coping with their baby's death.

> I never saw him or held him. Before the delivery the nurse
> asked me if I wanted a service, but I was in a state of
> panic. I couldn't relate to such finality, so I said, "No."
> They never asked me again. Now I wish they had. I regret
> not seeing him.
>
> —Karen

Gradually, as research has been done on the effects of miscarriage, stillbirth and infant death, health professionals have learned what parents have known all along: The death of a baby is a profound loss, and parents need to grieve this loss. To hold their baby before, during or after death is now seen as an opportunity to love and gather memories of the baby. Feeling sad, angry, helpless or lonely is now viewed as a healthy reaction associated with grief. Talking about the baby to someone who can listen is now considered therapeutic. At best, grieving parents are finally beginning to receive the respect and attention they deserve.

\*   \*   \*

> All the work to create this baby,
> summoning his soul from who knows where,
> all to end as ashes in a little box.
> I can't stand the endless goneness of him.
>
> —Claudia Putnam

## POINTS TO REMEMBER

- Many people find death difficult to talk about.
- People do not expect babies to die; for you, the death of your baby is a cruel violation of these expectations.
- Many people do not recognize the depth of your loss. You may be surprised by the intensity of your grief.
- Your baby's death is untimely, unfair and senseless.
- When your baby dies, you not only lose a child, but also your dreams, a part of yourself, a part of your future.
- The brevity of your baby's life can make grieving complex and painful. You can't get fully acquainted with this special child, and the lack of memories makes it harder to experience a *gradual* goodbye.
- A lack of mourning rituals and a lack of support from friends, family or healthcare professionals can make you feel desperately alone with your grief.
- In spite of all these barriers and difficulties, you *can* grieve and survive the death of your baby. Also remember you are not alone.

# 2

# Grieving and Emotional Recovery

A baby's death is a devastating loss. It represents an end to all the fantasies, hopes and dreams of what might have been. Whether or not the pregnancy was planned, whether it ended in miscarriage or stillbirth, whether the baby lived one hour or one year, parents need to grieve.

## GRIEVING: A BEWILDERING PROCESS

Grief encompasses a multitude of thoughts and emotions. Many people have little experience with grief, and most have never felt the emotional impact of losing a child. As a bereaved parent, you may experience a range of feelings. It can be impossible to predict how you will feel from day to day, or hour to hour. Your life seems hopelessly altered and uncertain. You may wonder if you are going crazy. Because grieving the death of a baby is a bewildering experience, it can help to learn about what to expect, what other bereaved parents have experienced. By knowing about the grieving process, you can be reassured that your emotions are valid and normal. By knowing that others have mourned similarly, you may feel less isolated and better able to cope with your grief.

> It would have helped if somebody had educated us and told us what it was going to be like and said, "You're going to feel these things. Don't think you're going crazy, because it's normal." I didn't know what was going on. So I thought I was going crazy and I didn't want to tell anybody about the feelings.
>
> —Desi

Perhaps one of the most important things to remember is that there is no right or wrong way to grieve, and there is no established length of time for the process. The bereaved parent who expects to feel a certain way after a certain amount of time will only be distressed to discover that grief is not so predictable.

Moreover, no two people grieve in the same way or with the same intensity. Different feelings surface at different times. During this stressful period, you need to remember that it is normal for you and your partner to grieve in unique, personal ways. Counseling and support groups can help you communicate more openly with each other about the baby and your sadness. Open communication will help you understand, support and comfort each other.

## THE GRIEF REACTION

Grief is a definite syndrome involving intense feelings of distress. There are a number of psychological symptoms:

- preoccupation with thoughts of the deceased
- irritability
- restlessness
- anxiety
- fear
- yearning
- hopelessness
- confusion

There are also a number of physical symptoms:

- shortness of breath
- tightness in the throat
- fatigue
- sighing
- crying spells
- empty feeling in the abdomen
- sleeplessness
- change in appetite
- heart palpitations and other manifestations of anxiety

These symptoms of intense distress can occur in waves lasting from several minutes to an hour. During these acute attacks, it's important to take time out to deal with the grief until activities can be resumed safely or attentively.

There may also be changes in personality brought out by emotional stress, anxiety and despair. A fastidious person may become careless; an outgoing person may become withdrawn; an even-tempered person may become quick to anger.

In addition to the above symptoms, many bereaved parents report empty, aching arms and illusions of seeing or feeling the presence of the baby. These intense symptoms may peak after several months, with variable peaks continuing for many months. Although many people expect grieving parents to recover and "get back to normal" within a few weeks or months, grief appears to be an open-ended process of recovery with no tangible ending. Parents gradually regain steady functioning, but many report that "back to normal" can take several years. Some parents feel that "back to normal" is an unrealistic goal, that this experience has changed them forever.

## UNDERSTANDING THE GRIEVING PROCESS

A common way to think about grief is in terms of stages to progress through after a loved one's death. These stages include (1) shock and numbness, (2) denial and searching-yearning, (3) anger, guilt and failure, (4) depression and disorganization and (5) resolution. Thinking about the grieving process in terms of these phases gives some organization to an otherwise bewildering emotional experience.

However, there are a number of disadvantages to thinking about grieving as progression through stages. For one thing, these stages are by no means distinct or irreversible. Progression through each phase can take days or months, even years, and at times grieving parents may vacillate from one to another. It is not at all uncommon for parents to feel numb one minute and angry the next, or to feel both denial and depression at the same time. Finally, by trying to adhere to "progression through the stages," parents can become discouraged when they notice that their progression is not smooth or timely.

It may be more helpful for parents to think of the grieving process as a more fluid experience of a variety of emotions with one underlying theme: coming to terms with the loss.

Throughout our lives, we form durable emotional attachments

to others. When a loved one dies, we feel deprived, reduced and resistant to the changes and adjustments that must be made. Grief is the painful price we pay for our heartfelt connections with others.

Because these relationships are so durable, we cannot immediately and fully confront the reality of a loved one's death. To do so would be emotionally overwhelming. Instead, we require a gradual goodbye in order to work through all the painful emotions and try to make sense of our loss. Many of the emotions of grief, including numbness, denial and anger, are forms of avoidance or protest. These allow us to adjust slowly to the death and the impact it has on our lives.

As you, the bereaved parent, work through these feelings, you may feel a growing realization that the baby is gone and what might have been cannot be recovered. As you confront reality, eventually you may feel a sense of resignation about your baby's death, and with that, a deep sadness and disorganization. Even so, you may still feel anger and even occasional denial as you fluctuate between yearning for the baby and saying goodbye. Eventually, as you adjust to the changes that your baby's death has wrought, you can reinvest your time and energy in regular activities and relationships. In this way you begin to reorganize your life and perhaps experience a renewing sense of acceptance and resolution.

Many parents have compared their grieving process to riding a roller coaster. Grieving is rarely a predictable or smooth progression toward resolution. As you weave through avoidance, protest, confrontation, resignation, adjustment and reestablishment, you will experience many ups and downs. At first the bad days will outnumber the good days. But as time goes on, the bad days will become less frequent and the good days will occur more often. After several years the downs may become less intense, but for many parents, the downs can remain as painful and intense as ever. This can be discouraging, but eventually you *will* have more prolonged ups and you *will* survive the downs.

> After a year, a surge of grief can be as hard as ever, but it only lasts a couple hours instead of days on end. ... It becomes slivers of pain. As time goes on it is still very painful but less consuming and less overwhelming, like you find a small place for it instead of it being your whole existence.
>
> —Claudia

# COMMON GRIEVING EMOTIONS

### NUMBNESS AND SHOCK

There will be times, especially right after the baby's death, when you may feel as though you are in shock. Even the fact of your baby's death may not register for several days, almost as if your mind tries to protect you from the awful reality. You may appear to be unaffected by this tragedy or taking it in stride, largely because it hasn't hit you yet. Throughout the months following the baby's death, you may still endure occasional periods when the baby's death seems unreal, but the pervasive numbness normally occurs during the weeks immediately following the death.

> The day James died I was very numb. It was very undramatic. I didn't start really feeling anything for a long time, for a couple of weeks, before I started to really hurt. It was like I was watching somebody else go through the whole thing. My husband fell apart and I watched myself go over and comfort him and I watched myself go for the next two weeks, feeling guilty as hell that I wasn't hysterical or that I was actually laughing. I watched myself do these things, but I wasn't a part of what was happening.
> —Sarah

> At first you're in shock and when you come out of it, then it hits you what happened and then you're back in shock again. I'd say the first two months were like that, and then it started easing up a little bit at a time.
> —Martina

Because feeling nothing at all is preferable to the pain of grief, numbness is a common way to avoid distress. However, in the long run, grief and pain cannot be avoided, only disguised. If you habitually avoid or repress grief, it will appear indirectly, in ways that may severely compromise your health and happiness. Avoidance or repression of grief may result in the following symptoms:

- physical illness, such as recurring viral or bacterial infections, fatigue, allergy sensitivity, aching muscles or joints

- overactivity, such as working overtime, keeping busy all the time, filling up the calendar with commitments, feeling restless
- anxiety, a vague, uncomfortable feeling of fear or dread, which may be accompanied by rapid breathing and heartbeat, nausea, diarrhea, headaches, sweating, irritability, insomnia, trembling, nightmares
- depression, including vague feelings of dissatisfaction, unhappiness, boredom, loss of interest in life, excessive sleeping or insomnia, difficulty concentrating or making decisions, intense guilt, irritability, crying spells
- disrupted relationships, such as troubled marriage, broken friendships, conflict in family relationships, isolation
- substance abuse, including alcohol, food, cigarettes, tranquilizers, other drugs
- other compulsive or addictive behaviors, such as engaging excessively in exercise, shopping, gambling, cleaning, sleeping, television watching, sexual activity
- violence, such as getting into verbal or physical fights with anyone, including family members; car accidents
- other self-destructive behaviors, such as lack of good judgment, accidents that might have been avoided if you had been normally cautious or alert

While occasional avoidance can help you cope by alleviating the intense pain of grief, a prevailing or continuing feeling of detachment may indicate that you are repressing grief to your detriment. If this is the case, you may benefit from counseling with a therapist who recognizes the importance of grieving and the significance of miscarriage, stillbirth and infant death. You may need to talk to someone who can help you gradually say goodbye, work through the pain and cope with your loss. (See "Counseling" in chapter 9.)

## DENIAL AND YEARNING

As the reality of your baby's death registers, shock and numbness subside. Periodically, however, you may find yourself believing that the baby is still alive. This is normal. For a while, you may wonder if this is all a bad dream and you'll wake up soon to find a healthy baby in your arms. If your doctor diagnosed miscarriage, you may wonder if the ultrasound simply failed to detect the fetal heartbeat within you. If the baby's death was diagnosed just before delivery, you may believe that you detected fetal movement and that the baby was indeed fine. You may feel a strong desire to retrieve your dead baby, wanting to resuscitate the lifeless body or wondering if the dead infant really belongs to someone else and that your baby is somewhere, alive and well.

> I did a lot of denial. I kept trying to believe all this really didn't happen and I kept hoping that I'd wake up tomorrow morning and everything would be all right. I felt like I was living in a nightmare. That lasted quite awhile.
>
> —Lena

> Even after she was stillborn, it was kind of a relief to finally have her in my arms. But then again, I wanted her to be awake and I wanted her to cry and I wanted her to act like a normal ... I wanted her to be alive. I really didn't realize she was dead until I held her. I mean, I kept thinking during labor, "maybe, maybe." Even after seeing that monitor and that line where her heartbeat should've been was just a solid line, I still didn't believe it. ... But my subconscious or me not wanting to believe the truth kept saying, "maybe she'll cry and everybody will be shocked." A few days later in the funeral home I kept thinking, 'Why don't you just wake up. Just wake up and cry. CRY and then we'll be all right, and I'll take you home!
>
> — Cindy

> I think everybody must have little fantasies that are a part of denial that help you. Sometimes I feel like he didn't die, that somehow someone else had become attached to him and they realized it was going to be hard to separate them. I know that this isn't true, but it's a little fantasy that keeps me going. So every once in a while I have that feeling that this is *so* unreal that that's what really happened, that someone else took him.
>
> —Liza

In yearning for your baby, you may feel totally preoccupied with thoughts of him or her. At times you may believe you hear the baby crying. When you peek into the nursery you may, for a split second, believe you see the baby lying in the bassinet. You may dream vividly about your baby. These illusions and dreams occur as part of a normal protest, but also enable you to gradually face the fact that your baby is gone.

## BLAMING YOURSELF, RESENTING OTHERS

As you squarely face your baby's death, you may experience feelings of failure, anger and guilt. These emotions are part of protesting and confronting the death. Feelings of failure tug at you as you wonder if you are able to produce a healthy baby. Diagnostic terms such as *genetic mutation, habitual aborter, irritable uterus, incompetent cervix* and *blighted ovum* can add to your discouragement. A sense of inadequacy, particularly for mothers, may arise from the idea that your body betrayed you, or that you are less of a woman or less of a mother because your baby died. Like many mothers, Kelly recalls, "I didn't feel I was a good mother, a good person, because I couldn't do this one thing right."

Bereaved mothers usually feel jealous toward pregnant women or mothers with infants. You may resent mothers who seem to effortlessly produce healthy babies despite abominable habits during pregnancy. You may bristle when you hear about abusive or neglecting parents. It's so unfair. You may also feel angry at fate, God, doctors or your partner as you search for reasons to explain your baby's death.

> All these women who don't even want their babies or the ones who don't take care of their bodies can pop them out with no problem and practically no medical care. How come I couldn't do it?
>
> —Desi

> I suppose I should say, "It's so unfair, but I don't wish other moms and babies harm." But oh, I do. I know it's not right and I don't want children to die, but I want those mothers to feel what I feel so I'm less isolated, so I'm not the only one. I am slightly disappointed when a healthy baby is born—they don't know how lucky they are.
>
> —Stephanie

My first feelings were like I'd been singled out or something. Why did God do this to me?

—Liza

Guilt is anger directed at the self. It is most apparent when you
wonder whether there was something you did or did not do that
caused your baby's death. Was it genetic or environmental? Did your
body betray you and contribute to your baby's death? Could you
have somehow prevented this? Did you do something to deserve this
awful tragedy? Bess remarks, "I thought maybe I was getting paid
back for something I did that was wrong."

> It was the guilt that I have a baby inside of me. I'm the
> only person that could hurt or help that baby. What I
> consume in my body is what goes to that kid, and I
> couldn't even know when something's wrong and I
> couldn't even act and get her out and take care of her. I
> mean, this is the inside of my body. That was the guilt. I
> just felt like people thought, "Well, gosh, she was inside
> of you; didn't you know something was wrong? Couldn't
> you tell?"
>
> —Cindy

Unfortunately, this self-directed anger can lead to self-destructive
behavior and chronic depression. It is natural and valid to feel anger,
but it is healthier to direct your rage at your doctor, nurses, fate, God,
insensitive people or even pregnant women, rather than yourself.
After all, you would never have done anything knowingly to hurt
your baby. You did the best you could.

> At first I thought, "You're not a woman anymore if you
> can't have a baby that lives. It's your fault." But it's not
> your fault. You go through guilt and then you realize
> finally that it wasn't you that did it. And then you try to
> blame it on everybody else. But I can remember blaming it
> on myself more than anything.
>
> —Martina

Failure, anger and guilt are very common but difficult feelings to cope with. We will examine these grieving feelings in more detail in chapter 6.

### DEPRESSION, DISORGANIZATION AND DESPAIR

As you grasp the fact that your baby is gone forever, you begin to adjust to the changes in your life. Naturally, you feel depressed and disorganized and extremely sad. You may feel apathetic and unable to enjoy your friends, hobbies or other pleasurable activities. You may feel pessimistic, hopeless, victimized, deprived, vulnerable and powerless.

> I got real depressed, which I'd never experienced. ... You know, everybody has days when they're down in the dumps, but I was why-even-get-out-of-bed depressed, where all I wanted to do was sleep. ... I just couldn't think of any reasons why I wanted to continue, that's how depressed I was.
>
> —Sarah

> Just any routine thing was like a major ordeal. It just seemed like your whole world had been totally turned upside down, and then to just go back to the mundane stuff like going to the grocery store when your baby had died, it was, like, what difference does it make?
>
> —Hannah

If you feel like your everyday functioning is impaired—that you lack energy, don't care anymore, can't concentrate or feel so disorganized that it is impossible to get much accomplished—realize that this is normal. Set aside time for yourself. Do things that don't require much energy or concentration. Make lists to help your memory and organization. If you can't handle much responsibility, have someone else take up the slack for a while.

> There are days where you wonder if you'll make it to the next day, and days where you don't even care if you do.
>
> —Claudia

> I went through a stage where I just didn't care. When it
> was time to pay a bill I thought, "Well, big deal, if it gets
> paid, fine, if it doesn't, fine." I mean, I didn't care about
> anything. Now I'm back to caring about certain things.
> But I went through that feeling that nothing is important
> anymore; I've lost what's important to me, so why should
> anything else be important?
>
> —Martina

If you become concerned about your depression, you may find it helpful to talk to someone. If your depression is due to an attempt to submerge your grief, a counselor can help you get back in touch with your feelings so you can cope with them more constructively. A counselor can encourage you to express your sadness, anger and disappointment, and help you adjust to a new relationship with your baby.

# THE BITTERSWEET PATH
# TO RESOLUTION

You will never forget your baby. Many people mistakenly believe that resolution means you stop grieving, forget about the baby and meekly abandon your baby to death. To the contrary, grief does not end. You will always feel some sadness and wish things could have turned out better. But with time, the denial, failure, guilt and anger fade; the sadness becomes manageable. You haven't surrendered your baby. Instead, your relationship to the baby has changed. You learn to accept it and integrate the experience into your life. Your memories of the baby are not idealized and can evoke pleasant emotions. As you remember your baby fondly, thoughts become bittersweet: sadness merges with your happier memories, and you acquire a sense of peace.

> Her life and death feel like a very integrated part of my
> life right now and not something that I could or would
> change, just something that happened and I'm going to
> cope with it. I don't feel as though it's limiting anymore,
> it's just part of my life.
>
> —Jessie

When I think about it, it's always going to be sad. I can look back on the time we had with him, and although it was the only time we'll ever have with him, I can smile. I didn't think I'd ever smile. Every time I thought about that, it would make me cry. It doesn't make me cry anymore. Now it makes me real grateful that I had that time. I feel really, really grateful that I had him for three days. And I didn't think I'd ever feel that way.

—Sarah

Resolution takes time. Of the mothers in this book, most needed more than four years to feel resolved. Some mothers needed less time, some mothers needed more. Some mothers still do not consider themselves resolved. They continue to feel intense sadness many years after their baby's death.

It will always be there, I'm sure. Even in fifty years I'll still remember. I'm not grieving like you do right afterwards. But I still have sadness and pain. It still bothers me, but not every day.

—Rayleen

How do I feel now, seven years later? That there is a missing part in our life, that the family is incomplete. … I still miss him and I don't know that that ever goes away. It's less now—it used to be every minute of every day and then it was just a few days a week and then a few weeks in the month. Sometimes I'll be like this only once in a year. Sometimes it's worse and sometimes it's not. I just wish it had never happened, never, ever, ever.

—Bess

The peaceful feelings that come with resolution are a blessed change from the ravages of grief, and most parents hope to find some resolution. Chapter 7 looks at resolution in more detail and describes how some mothers have integrated their babies' deaths into their lives.

# SURVIVING GRIEF

It's important to remember that people grieve in different ways. Not everyone will feel guilt, failure, loneliness or deep depression. No one will feel like that all the time. Your grief may be intense or gentle, overwhelming or manageable, somewhere in between or vacillating between extremes.

It's also important to remember that the only way to work your way through grief is to acknowledge all of your feelings. However painful this may be, it's the only way, and in the long run, acknowledging is actually less harmful than repressing or avoiding grief. In fact, experts in bereavement agree that *the quality of your grief work can determine the quality of your life.* By experiencing and dealing with your emotions, you increase your chances of healing and of finding peace and happiness again. Suppressing feelings increases distress.

Many parents benefit from attending bereaved parent support groups, as well as individual counseling. Both resources offer a place where you can express your feelings. If you feel stuck, overwhelmed, at the end of your rope, that your life and relationships are unraveling, or if you feel nothing at all for longer than you think you should, you may benefit from talking to a counselor. Doing so may help you work through your grief toward resolution. Seeking help is a sign of strength. You deserve to feel better. Your doctor, local community mental health clinic, support group leaders, hospital social worker or psychologist, hospice organization, grief institute or other bereaved parents may be able to refer you to someone to talk with. (See chapter 9 and appendix B, "Resources for Bereaved Parents.")

## POINTS TO REMEMBER

- Grieving is a process of coming to terms with your loss—trying to make sense of it and gradually saying goodbye.
- Grief includes a broad range of emotions.
- Many other parents have felt these same powerful feelings, but all people grieve in their own personal way, with their own intensity, on their own timetable.
- Grief cannot be avoided, only delayed or disguised.
- You are entitled to your feelings; give yourself permission to feel them. The quality of your grief work will determine your chances for healing and finding peace.
- Grieving is a process that takes time.
- Be kind to yourself as you make this journey through grief.
- You will survive.

# 3

# Physical Recovery

I felt a real physical loss because she was attached to me for her whole life—then she was gone. And then I had all this milk and there was no baby. I felt as though a part of me had just been cut out, a real overwhelming, intense sadness.

—Jessie

When your baby dies, not only do you feel emotionally devastated, you may also feel physically devastated. Many mothers report fatigue, insomnia, and empty, aching arms. If your baby died in the womb or shortly after birth, you have all the signs of pregnancy and giving birth, but no baby. Your emotional load can be further increased by postpartum depression, caused by the natural readjustment of your hormones to nonpregnant levels. This period may last several weeks and accounts for some of your mood swings and mothering urges. If your baby died while you were still breast-feeding (or getting ready to breast-feed), you must also cope with your breasts as they continue to produce milk.

These cruel twists of nature can make your physical recovery very painful. You may feel angry at your body or impatient for the signs of childbirth or breast-feeding to disappear. It seems so unfair. But with time and by taking care of your body, you will soon recover physically. Good nutrition, rest and emotional support can lessen the fatigue, anxiety and depression normally associated with postpartum recovery. After you feel better physically, you may find that you are better able to cope with your grief and focus on your emotional recovery.

This postpartum information is adapted for bereaved mothers. All parents may find useful information in the sections on sex, contraception, fatigue, sleep, employment, diet, exercise and relaxation. Although based on sound medical judgment, this information should be used in conjunction with advice given by your doctor, as well as your own common sense. Your doctor can make more specific recommendations based on your special condition and requirements. Always consult your doctor if you have worrisome or complicating problems.

# BREAST CARE

In addition to physical discomfort, engorged breasts can make you feel emotionally distressed. If you planned on breast-feeding your baby, your sadness or anger is only heightened—here you are, beautifully equipped by nature to feed and nurture your baby, but there is no baby. Many mothers report that this is a very difficult part of postpartum physical recovery. If you have been breast-feeding, you may deeply miss this nurturing, loving act with your baby.

Your body produces milk because of the hormones in your bloodstream after delivery. Your breasts feel full and uncomfortable when you stop breast-feeding or when your milk comes in the second or third day after delivery. This engorgement period lasts up to forty-eight hours. Engorgement is caused by the pressure of fluid, which prevents further milk production. If you pump your breasts, the relief is only temporary as this signals your body to step up milk production.

If you wait it out while the milk is absorbed by your body, your breasts will soften gradually. Binding your breasts tightly or wearing a snug bra at all times should reduce discomfort. Ice packs on your breasts may also help, as the cold reduces swelling. A five-day regimen of vitamin $B^6$ in two-hundred-milligram doses has been shown to reduce engorgement. Relief can occur in about eleven hours. When your breasts are most swollen, you can also try kneeling in a hot bath with your breasts suspended in the water. The heat allows the milk to flow out without providing the stimulation that increases milk production.

It was the third day after my baby was stillborn. My milk had just come in and I had forgotten that was going to happen and I thought, "Oh, is this another torture thing here?" My sister had a baby and she couldn't breast-feed, and here I was with all this milk.

—Elaine

I've never been so empty in my life. I pictured breast-feeding him, I pictured him just laying in bed with us. I woke up in the middle of the night, wanting to get up to nurse him.

—Meryl

Call your doctor if you notice any signs of breast infection:

- any red, warm, hard or tender areas in your breasts
- fever above 100 degrees
- general ill feeling
- tender lymph glands in the underarm area

# DILATION & CURETTAGE
# (D & C)

If you had a D & C, you may feel a sense of violation. After the doctor determined that miscarriage was imminent, you may have wished that you had been allowed to go home and let nature take its course. If an incomplete miscarriage was diagnosed, you may have needed more time to adjust to your loss before this stark and final action. If you had a therapeutic abortion (by D & C or another procedure), you may feel especially violated by this intrusion into your body. If a curettage was performed to remove placental fragments and stop you from hemorrhaging, you may have feared for your life or your fertility.

You need to allow four to six weeks for physical recovery. During this period you can expect to tire easily. Your hormones may also be out of balance, which can make you feel extra moody or depressed. Check with your doctor about restrictions on driving and other activity. To reduce chances of infection and to promote healing of your cervix, avoid intercourse or using douches, tampons or menstrual sponges. For additional information, consult "Uterine Healing" later in this chapter.

Call your doctor if you notice any signs of infection or complications:

- pain that is not alleviated by non-prescription pain relievers such as aspirin, ibuprofen or acetaminophen
- vaginal discharge that increases or smells unpleasant
- unusual vaginal swelling or heavy bleeding
- headache or muscle aches
- dizziness or general ill feeling
- fever above 100 degrees

## CESAREAN DELIVERY

If you had a Cesarean birth, you may feel additional grief over the disappointment that you could not deliver your baby vaginally. Or you may wonder why Cesarean delivery was not carried out sooner to save your baby's life. You may feel that a very invasive procedure was done to your body, all for naught. In any case, your body must recover without benefit of a baby in your arms.

It is important to remember that you are recovering from major surgery. Your body needs about six weeks to heal completely. You may tire easily for several months after delivery. Walking or standing for long periods of time can be exhausting. Give yourself time to heal before you resume your normal activities. Check with your doctor about specific activity restrictions. Restrictions often include lifting anything heavier than twenty pounds, mopping and vacuuming. Do not drive during the first one or two weeks, since your reaction time is slower.

You need to examine your incision every day to make sure it is healing properly. If your doctor used steri-strips, you should leave them on your incision until they start peeling off on their own. Check with your doctor about bathing. For additional information, consult the next section "Uterine Healing."

Call your doctor if you notice the edges of the incision coming apart, or any signs of infection:

- increased pain or tenderness
- increased swelling or reddened skin around the incision
- fluid or discharge from the incision

- fever above 100 degrees
- continuing urge to urinate frequently

# UTERINE HEALING

Vaginal bleeding is normal for up to ten days after miscarriage and eight weeks after delivery. The flow is called "lochia" and consists of the lining of your uterus and blood from where the placenta was attached to your uterine wall. Over time the color changes from red to pink or brown to whitish-yellow. Occasionally you may notice clots, up to the size of a quarter. You may also notice an increase in flow when you stand up or engage in vigorous physical activity. Within seven to twenty one days after delivery, the clotted area at the placental site loosens, and you may notice more bleeding for a few days. In general, increased bleeding is a signal that you need to slow your activity, get more rest and drink lots of fluids. To reduce chances of infection, avoid vaginal penetration, including intercourse, tampons or douches, for at least four weeks. Your uterus will need four to six weeks to heal and return to its normal size and position and for the cervix to close.

Watch for symptoms that may indicate infection or abnormal bleeding. Call your doctor if you have any concerns or if you notice any of the following:

- bleeding that saturates one or more sanitary pads in an hour
- dizziness or lightheadedness, particularly with heavier bleeding
- vaginal flow or discharge that smells unpleasant
- fever above 100 degrees
- pain or burning with urination
- red, warm or tender areas in your breasts or legs
- general ill feeling or any new symptoms of discomfort

# EPISIOTOMY CARE

An episiotomy heals and the stitches dissolve in about three to six weeks. To prevent infection, keep the area clean by rinsing with warm water after going to the bathroom and by always wiping from front to back. Change your pad every two hours or less. To relieve soreness and promote healing, sit in a shallow amount of clean water two to four times a day for about fifteen minutes. Use warm or cold water, whichever relieves your discomfort. You might also try sitting on a donut-shaped pillow, or squeezing your buttocks together before sitting and using ice packs, anesthetic sprays, ointments, witch hazel pads (Tucks) or pain medication prescribed by your doctor.

Call your doctor if you notice any signs of complications or infection:

- any increase in pain, swelling, redness, drainage or bleeding around the incision
- headache, muscle aches, dizziness or general ill feeling
- nausea, vomiting, constipation or abdominal swelling
- fever above 100 degrees

## POSTPARTUM VISITS

About six weeks after delivery, your doctor will want to give you a pelvic exam and check your general physical condition, your urine, your breasts and your abdominal wall. These exams enable your doctor to make sure your body is healing properly. You may want to make another appointment prior to the six-week checkup, to ask questions and learn more about what happened. Because doctors' offices are generally full of pregnant women and mothers with infants, you may want to ask for the first or last appointment of the day. Many bereaved mothers find it too painful to be around pregnant women and babies. If sitting in the waiting room would make you feel uncomfortable, explain your situation when you arrive, and ask the receptionist to seat you in an exam room.

## SEX AND CONTRACEPTION

Parents vary on their interest in sex after their baby dies. For some parents, sex provides the intimacy they want, while for other parents, it seems like a worthless or painful activity, especially when associated with conception. When you are intensely grieving or if your relationship is stressed, you may feel too emotionally drained.

Fatigue, soreness and hormonal changes may also affect your

interest in sex. Your doctor may advise you to avoid any vaginal penetration until your healing is checked at the six-week postpartum exam. Physically, you are able to resume intercourse when your bleeding stops and when you feel comfortable with penetration. It is important to be gentle during intercourse the first few times. A water-soluble lubricant (such as K-Y Jelly) may be helpful in reducing discomfort. Try different positions to minimize discomfort caused by pressure on your episiotomy or other tender areas. You can also try other ways to express sexual intimacy and physical affection. (See chapter 8 for more information on couples and sex.)

Many mothers long to be pregnant again immediately, but if you are still recovering from pregnancy, you need time to heal physically. To avoid conception, you need to use birth control as soon as you resume intercourse. Pregnancy can occur before your menstrual period reappears, as the first ovulation can happen anytime. The refitting of a diaphragm is necessary after each pregnancy due to changes in the size of the cervix. In addition, a diaphragm needs to be fitted after the six-week period during which the uterus and cervix return to their normal size and position. Other birth control methods can be adopted immediately, including condoms and foam. Discuss birth control with your doctor to find the method that is right for you.

> At first, birth control was just out of the question. I just couldn't use anything, I just *couldn't*! Then, after a couple months, I decided I was feeling a little bit better, and I wasn't going to risk any more pain. But at about the time we decided we weren't going to have any more children, I discovered I was pregnant.
>
> —Sarah

Whether you are still recovering from pregnancy or not, you need time to think about this important decision. (See chapter 10 for more information on timing another pregnancy.)

## FATIGUE AND SLEEP

After pregnancy, including one cut short by miscarriage, a bereaved mother's fatigue is different from that of other postpartum mothers. Any comparisons are unfair because grief contributes immeasurably to the fatigue of recovering from pregnancy. If your baby died after your postpartum period, fatigue is still a common symptom of grief.

> A lot of times I would just sit and either write or just close my eyes for hours. There were a few times I couldn't even get up. I would try to make dinner and my arms would be so heavy—there would be no energy. I couldn't even push the spatula in the pan. I just was like, "I don't care, I'm not hungry." I felt real sick in my stomach. I couldn't even breathe right. It was just like big sighs.
>
> —Rose

> The biggest thing I remember was empty arms. My arms just ached. I've read about this and it's hard to believe, but to me there was actually a physical emptiness. I could almost feel my arms cradling, but there wasn't anything there.
>
> —Meryl

Trying to take on too much too soon can exhaust you and prevent your physical or emotional healing. This is a time to take it easy and do what's best for you. The following suggestions may help reduce fatigue and thereby increase your ability to cope with your grief as well as manage the activities of everyday life.

- Let others help, or hire someone to do the household chores, the cooking and the childcare for any other children you may have.
- Do essential housework and errands during the part of the day when you feel most energetic.
- Keep meals simple; limit housekeeping to a minimum.
- Sleep or rest whenever you find the opportunity; don't limit your relaxing hours to nighttime. You may find that you don't always get enough rest in those hours you set aside.

It is very common for grieving parents to experience sleep disturbances. You may fall into bed exhausted, only to be consumed with thoughts, regrets and grief about your baby. Or you may waken in the middle of the night, unable to get back to sleep. Especially if you are very busy during the day, nighttime may be when your mind demands the time to grieve.

An *occasional* sedative prescribed by your doctor can help you get much-needed sleep, but beware of using medication (or alcohol or other drugs) to avoid the pain of grief. Anesthetizing yourself does not get rid of the feelings—it only increases their pressure and power inside you, making them more volatile and painful to deal with in the long run.

Some bereaved parents notice that they sleep more, not less. Additional sleep may give you the energy you need for the hard work of grieving. However, excessive sleep can be a way of avoiding grief by providing the same escape as anesthetizing yourself with drugs or alcohol. Both insomnia and excessive sleep are also common symptoms of depression. If either problem is prolonged or concerns you, seek out counseling or support groups to help you cope with your grief.

> I had trouble sleeping for awhile. I'd wake up in the night after I had her—I'd try to listen for something, and that lasted for months.
>
> —Erin

For many parents, sleep irregularities are temporary or occasional. You can try inducing healthful sleep with the following ideas.

- Give yourself opportunities during the day to grieve and think about your baby.
- Keep a journal. Write down your thoughts and feelings— putting them on paper releases them from circulating in your mind. Try doing this during the day; it can also help during a restless night.
- Exercise during the day. This can help you to feel more relaxed at bedtime and to sleep more soundly.
- Remind yourself that you deserve the respite of sleep and tranquility.
- Set aside time in the evening for winding down with a warm bath or other passive activity. Avoid caffeine (including soft drinks and chocolate), nicotine and other stimulants. Alcohol can also interfere with normal sleep patterns.

- If you fall asleep to music, have an automatic timer turn it off. Research indicates you can sleep more deeply in silence.
- Practice relaxation techniques at bedtime and when you wake up in the night. For instance, close your eyes and think of gentle, downward movement. Picture yourself floating down like a feather from the sky or gliding down stairs or descending in the elevator of a skyscraper. (For more techniques, see "Relaxation" later in this chapter.)

# EMPLOYMENT

If you were employed outside the home before the baby died, you may feel pressure to give up maternity leave and return to work. Instead, consider taking a leave of absence—as much as you can afford—for emotional and physical recovery. For some mothers, returning to work gives them a sense of worth, something to do, a way to be with people. Other mothers prefer not to resume their jobs. They may worry that they would be unable to concentrate on their work or lack the energy to put in the necessary effort. They may prefer to be alone with their thoughts and their grief. The thought of having more things to do may feel overwhelming. Your decision may depend on whether your job is normally a stressful one and whether you find balancing job and family difficult, as many mothers do. Remember, adjusting to the death of your baby has already put you under a tremendous amount of stress. To make a decision about returning to work, consider your physical and emotional needs and how you can best fulfill them.

# DIET AND EXERCISE

Ask your doctor if you have any special dietary needs. You may have little interest in food, or you may feel like eating foods that are not particularly nutritious. Because you are under stress, be sure to eat enough protein, vitamins and minerals, especially the B and C vitamins, iron and zinc. Drink plenty of water to keep your body functioning smoothly. Many mothers are concerned about regaining their normal figures after pregnancy. You may feel impatient about losing weight, but find it difficult to diet. Diets make the dieter feel deprived, and you may not want to add to the feelings of deprivation you already have over the death of your baby. Many mothers discover that it is more helpful to avoid dieting than to lose weight quickly. With time and good nutrition you will feel better emotionally and physically, and eventually your body will return to normal.

Ask your doctor if you should follow any exercise restrictions. You may feel as though you don't have the energy to exercise, but even a walk around the block can help clear your mind and get your body back in shape. Many mothers notice that physical activity helps reduce the stress of grieving. A bicycle ride can lift some depression; hitting a tennis ball against a backboard can be a good outlet for anger. To release tension or anxiety, try swimming, walking, jogging, aerobics, yoga, dancing, even gardening or housework. For losing weight, exercise is more effective than cutting calories because it keeps your body's metabolism humming along. Once you discover that exercise feels good, you may find it more appealing.

# RELAXATION

Along with nutrition and exercise, relaxation can help you reduce fatigue, anxiety or insomnia. Relaxation also enables your body to put its resources into healing. There are a number of good books and audiotapes on progressive relaxation techniques, including yoga. The basic idea is to make your body relax by consciously releasing muscle tension and by using imagery to put you in a relaxed state of mind. To release muscle tension, lie down so you are comfortable and all your body weight is supported. Relax your facial muscles, your jaw, your eyes, your brow. Starting with your toes, slowly work your way up to your scalp, relaxing each body part. Make your toes limp, then your ankles, calves, knees, thighs and so on. You can also concentrate on breathing slowly.

To add imagery, close your eyes and imagine a place that makes you feel peaceful. A sandy beach, a mountain lake, a flowery meadow, a grassy prairie, an evergreen forest. Picture a soft breeze, puffy clouds, brilliant colors, cool water, whispering pines, whatever pleases you. This is a place you can always go to if you want to feel relaxed and at peace. You can also try turning on some soothing music. New Age and Native American flute music have very soothing qualities. You deserve to take time out to relax.

## POINTS TO REMEMBER

- Establish your own timetable for postpartum recovery.
- Take care of your body as a way to help you cope with your grief.
- Give yourself a few months to decide about another pregnancy.
- Practice relaxation techniques to help you cope with fatigue, insomnia and anxiety.
- Give yourself opportunities to grieve and think about your baby, especially during the day.
- Be sensitive to your own special needs for sleep, nutrition, exercise, relaxation and sexual intimacy.

# 4

# The Early Months

## MAKING DIFFICULT DECISIONS

Around the time your baby died, you may have made many difficult decisions—choices that you never imagined having to make. Perhaps you were faced with decisions about terminating your pregnancy. If your health was in danger, you may have had to decide whether to terminate the pregnancy or risk grave illness, permanent impairment, even death. If your baby was diagnosed in utero with a disabling or fatal condition, you may have had to decide whether to spare your baby from a miserable, short life, or hope for the best. If your doctor determined that your baby was dead before birth, you may have had to decide whether to induce labor or go home and wait for labor to begin.

Perhaps you were faced with decisions about premature delivery. If your health or the baby's health was endangered, the risks of continuing the pregnancy versus the risks of your baby's prematurity had to be considered. If your baby sustained brain damage before, during or after birth, you may have had to face the decision of refusing life support. You may have had to decide whether the baby should be resuscitated, allowed to stop breathing naturally or allowed to go into cardiac arrest. If your baby was born with a serious birth defect, you may have had to decide whether to let your baby die quickly and naturally, or to risk life-threatening or possibly unsuccessful surgeries. Perhaps you had to decide when to stop further treatment or when to disconnect life-support systems.

### CHOOSING BETWEEN TERRIBLE AND HORRIBLE
None of these decisions involve much of a choice. It's as though you

had to choose between "terrible" and "horrible." You may feel guilty about your choice, and since you feel so bad you wonder, "Would the other choice have been better?" But really, you feel bad not because you made a *bad* decision, but because you had to make a tough, *painful* decision. Moreover, none of your options offered a total solution. Each one held its own risks and created its own problems. Most likely, you would feel equally bad or worse if you had chosen the alternative.

You may wonder later, "If I had had more time, would I have made a different choice?" But even with all the time in the world, you may still have made the same choice. Just remember that you made the best decision you possibly could—under terrible stress—weighing all the information at hand and balancing many factors, including your well-being and the welfare of your baby, your marriage and your other children.

You may feel obsessed by "What If?" for a while. This is another part of the grieving process. At some point, you might try focusing your energy on adjusting to the decisions you made, rather than wondering about what might have been. Instead of being angry at yourself for the decisions you made, be angry that you were put in the position to make a choice between "terrible" and "horrible."

Although you may wish someone could have made these difficult decisions for you, parents who are not given choices often regret it. As recently as ten years ago it was common hospital practice to not let parents have many options—from whether the mother stayed on the maternity floor to resuscitation orders to whether the parents were allowed to hold their baby. What happened often depended on hospital staff opinions and preferences. Most hospitals now realize that instead of being told what to do, parents need to be given alternatives, as well as enough information, support and time to make the right decisions for themselves.

There are several reasons why you, the parents, benefit from making your own decisions:

- You have unique emotional and spiritual needs. What may be right for another parent is not necessarily right for you.
- In the midst of tragedy, you may feel so helpless and ineffective. Having choices over what happens to you

and the baby can help reinstate your sense of control and self-esteem.

- It is you, not the hospital staff, who must live with the decisions that are made, for years to come.

### WRESTLING WITH LIFE AND DEATH DECISIONS

Before your baby died, you may have had to make decisions about medical treatments. To make a truly informed decision, you needed a lot of information about quality of life issues—how much the baby might suffer physically or emotionally (from the illness or the treatment), the physical health of the mother, and the emotional, financial and logistical difficulties in each choice. For example, if you had to decide whether to pursue treatment for a life-threatening disease or birth defect, you needed to know how difficult it would be for the baby. How painful would the treatment be? How long would it take? What were the chances it would be successful? What would the baby's quality of life be in the near future? In the distant future? Are some fates worse than death?

To judge what was best for your baby, you needed to weigh these risks and benefits. You also needed to know the logistics of obtaining experimental treatments and caring for a critically ill infant, particularly if it would have required hospitalization in a distant city. The financial realities, short–term and long–term, needed to be considered. Finally, you needed to think about the emotional consequences and strain on your marriage and other children. Considering all these factors can be difficult and confusing, and you may feel very angry if you learn that you did not receive critical information.

As much time as possible is needed to make such complex decisions. It can be very difficult for you to think clearly or quickly about such difficult choices. Sometimes, decisions must be made in a matter of moments. If this happened to you, you may have chosen to rely on your gut reaction or your doctor's advice. Again, you made the best decision you could, given your circumstances.

Each of the following parents wrestled with life and death decisions: Ruth suffers from hyperemesis gravidarum—severe nausea and vomiting throughout her pregnancies; Lena's baby was born 15 weeks early and died within a few hours; Claudia and John's baby was born with hypoplastic left heart syndrome and died three and a half days later.

I get very sick when I'm pregnant and with my last pregnancy, I was the sickest. I threw up every fifteen minutes around the clock. They tried IVs, but I was so dehydrated, they couldn't get them in. Finally, at nine weeks, I felt like I was dying and they really couldn't give me any answers and they didn't know if the baby would make it. So the doctors and my family really pressured me into terminating the pregnancy. I wish that they had given me a little more time to think about this decision, but they started things going right when I said, "Well, maybe we should. ... " But as time passes and I get more information, I can see that I may not have survived this pregnancy with the treatment I was getting. The way things were, how could I expect to keep going?

—Ruth

For quite a while I wondered if we did the right thing taking Stephen off life support. I thought "Gee, could he have been saved and lived a normal life?" They said most likely he would be mentally retarded and have cerebral palsy and he'd be a sick little child all of his life. Part of it was a little bit selfish—I didn't want to deal with that all my life. I do often wonder, though, what would've happened. Letting Stephen go for it on his own was probably the hardest decision I have faced or ever will face. But I wouldn't change that decision.

—Lena

We considered surgery, heart transplants, but at best these were risky, experimental procedures and babies haven't survived long enough for them to know about long-term quality of life. We knew that a life of pain and living in hospitals was not the life we wanted for Jacob. It was a painful decision, but we wanted him to know he was loved.

—Claudia

*DECISIONS AFTER YOUR BABY'S DEATH*
After a baby dies, most parents must make the difficult decisions of

whether to give consent for autopsy and whether to cremate or bury the baby's body or let the hospital handle it. Although painful, these decisions can give parents a sense of control and the chance to make arrangements that hold meaning for them.

Depending on how your baby died, you may not always be given choices. If you suffered a miscarriage in the hospital, they may dispose of the remains unless you insist on your right to keep them. If your baby died of SIDS or other accidental death, an autopsy may be required by law. Unfortunately, decisions made without your consent can enhance your feelings of powerlessness.

### Autopsy

You may be encouraged or required to give consent for an autopsy to determine the cause of your baby's death. Because of your natural, protective urges, giving permission for an autopsy can be very painful, especially if you don't like the idea of this invasion on your baby's body. If your baby was bombarded with wires and tubes and needles, the idea of the baby suffering any more may be unbearable, even though you know he or she cannot feel any more pain.

If the baby died of a specific known cause such as a heart defect, your doctor may suggest that only that specific part of the baby's body needs to be examined. In the case of stillbirth or newborn death, examination of the placenta and umbilical cord may yield important information. You may be comforted by the idea that an autopsy may add to medical knowledge that will help other babies, or that an autopsy will give you information that will increase your chances of having a healthy baby in the future. Or you may decide to refuse consent, in which case your doctor should respect this decision.

If you give consent for an autopsy, you may anxiously await the results. If you need results sooner to ease your mind, ask your doctor about this. After the autopsy is completed, you will probably want to discuss the results with your doctor, have your questions answered and even have a copy of the autopsy report. For many parents, the autopsy report is another memento, tangible evidence that the baby existed. For others, it's just an impersonal scientific report.

Unfortunately, autopsies don't always yield the exact cause of death. Especially in miscarried and stillborn babies, the cause of death is often unknown. If your baby died of SIDS, you will receive no answers about causes or prevention.

In any case, try to remember that the baby's death was not your fault. People like to think they have control over their bodies and their lives, but the scary truth is, they don't always. Sometimes bad things happen in random ways. It may take awhile to believe this, but anger at yourself for what happened to your baby is anger better directed at fate, God, genes, medical science or Mother Nature.

> I think the autopsy helped a lot because if you don't have a reason, it makes it harder to go on, and you never know whether the next baby is going to have the same problem. But if you have an autopsy, you know what was wrong.
>
> —Martina

> I really needed answers, but the autopsy couldn't tell why she stopped breathing inside of me. At first I really felt it was my fault because I carried that baby for nine months. So I thought I'd done something wrong, but I couldn't figure out what. I have no answers.
>
> —Erin

> They lost the autopsy results! That was a problem in that there was no completion as far as that goes. I never had an answer that I could completely rely on, but I know that that's the case a lot of times anyway. It took awhile to work through those feelings.
>
> —Anya

### Burial or Cremation

You may find it difficult to choose between the options of burial or cremation, as neither is a comforting thought. Some parents feel bad at the thought of their baby in the cold ground, and others can't imagine reducing their baby's body to ashes. Even though the baby is dead, your desire that he or she be comfortable is quite normal, and these feelings should be respected.

Some parents feel that the hospital or family pressured them to make decisions before they were ready. Martina remembers that she and her husband were expected to make these decisions right after their baby was stillborn. She points out, "They ask you those questions so soon and they don't realize you're not all there. When they asked me what I wanted to do with his body, I looked at my husband and he looked at me and we were stunned. 'What are you asking us this for right now? We don't want to talk about his *body*. He's our *son!*' "

Whenever possible, parents should be given as much time as they need to make this difficult decision. Anya remembers, "I wasn't ready to make a decision for more than a week. I wanted to check out funeral homes and visit cemeteries and I was very grateful that the hospital didn't pressure me. I could wait until I was ready. I felt like this was a decision I had to live with for the rest of my life and I didn't want to be forced to make a snap judgment."

Money is often an issue. Some parents don't have the money to spend and others are outraged at the principle of having to pay a lot of money for a tiny casket or the injustice of paying all this money and not having a healthy baby in their arms. There are funeral homes that provide free services for infants, but unless your hospital refers you, you may not have the knowledge or energy to track down this information. Some parents elect to use free hospital services—the hospital arranges cremation at a local mortuary, but then there is no way to obtain the ashes. Unfortunately, many parents later discover that they would feel comfort in knowing where the baby is. Erin observes, "We've always wondered if we did the right thing because we've driven out to the cemetery and the hospital babies, stillborns, are all together. We put flowers out there, not knowing where she was. ..."

It is normal to wonder what you might have done differently or how it might have eased the pain. Remember, your decisions were based on your circumstances, needs and options given at the time; if you suffered a miscarriage or stillbirth, you may not have been offered any options.

If you feel you were denied adequate choices, time or information to make some of these difficult decisions, you may consider talking to your doctor about this. (See chapter 5 for more information about decisions concerning cremation/burial and funeral/memorial services.)

## BEWILDERING FEELINGS

Grieving poses many questions, especially in the beginning.

- Will I survive this tragedy?

- What is this grieving process? How do I get through it?
- What will I feel tomorrow, next week, next month, next year?
- Are my feelings and behaviors normal?
- Will I feel better, ever?

In time, you will find some answers to these questions. For instance, yes, you will survive this, and in doing so, you may feel you can survive anything life presents.

What will you feel tomorrow, next week, next month, next year? Grief is unpredictable. You will know what you feel when you get there. Since no two people grieve exactly alike, you must find your own path through grief.

One thing is certain: you can disguise grief, but you cannot avoid it. If you try to avoid your feelings of sadness, anger and hurt, you will compromise other areas of your life. For instance, you may find yourself having difficulties at work or in your relationships. You may feel embittered, angry, that others are "out to get you." You may shut off all your feelings so you can honestly say you feel nothing at all— about anything. You may engage in compulsive behaviors, such as overeating, overspending money or extramarital affairs. You may rely on alcohol, tobacco or drugs. You may work all the time, dive into volunteer activities or keep the house immaculately clean. While you may feel that you are successfully distracting yourself from grief, you are actually a prisoner of your grief. To free yourself, you can't go over it, you can't go under it, you can't go around it, you just have to go through it.

Going through grief is painful, but you will gradually feel better as the months and years go by. If you take the time to grieve and avoid placing expectations on yourself to feel better at a certain time, you will work through your grief more easily than if you try to forget about it or pressure yourself to get over it quickly. Remember that grief is not a sign of weakness, rather, it takes strength and courage to acknowledge your emotions. This is a time to listen to your feelings, to nurture yourself, to value yourself, to get the emotional support you need.

Grief is also bewildering, and at times you may not know whether you are coming or going. You may worry about whether your feelings and behaviors are normal. You may wonder if you or your partner are doing OK. The following questions are shared by many grieving parents.

## IS IT NORMAL TO FEEL CRAZY?

Because grieving can be such a powerful experience, full of bewildering and unpredictable emotions, many parents wonder if they are going crazy. However, since most parents experience these overwhelming feelings, they must be a normal part of grieving.

Some of the common disturbances parents experience include insomnia, lack of concentration, forgetfulness, confusion, illusions of hearing or seeing the baby, feeling short-tempered and feeling suicidal.

Talking to someone about these feelings can help you handle them. While these reactions are normal, they do range from benign to serious. It may help just to be able to talk to a supportive friend, family member or another bereaved parent, someone who can really listen and let you express your thoughts and feelings. If you have some concerns about your feelings or your behavior, or if you are feeling overwhelmed or "stuck," it may be helpful for you to talk to a professional. Contact your doctor, local community mental health clinic, hospital social worker, support group leader or hospice organization. These professionals may also refer you to a counselor who understands bereavement. Talking can help you to work through your powerful emotions and to gain reassurance that your feelings are quite normal and reasonable. Remember, grieving is hard work and takes a lot of energy.

> It was hard going on with the daily living, all the little stuff. There wasn't a lot of sense to it for a while. I remember distinctly feeling like I was losing my mind.
>
> —Bess

> I tried to leave the hospital by way of jumping out the window. I can remember doing things like that, just trying to get away from it, thinking, "Now if I leave the hospital, everything will be okay." It just seems like your mind ... you can really be a sane person, but when something like that happens, you just lose it.
>
> —Martina

I knew that it wasn't crazy to feel crazy, but even though I
had that understanding, it was helpful to have people
around me who would say, "That's normal, it's OK to
feel that way, let yourself feel that way."

—Sophie

## IS IT NORMAL TO FEEL SOME RELIEF
## UPON MY BABY'S DEATH?

When parents know ahead of time that death is possible or inevitable,
they can begin to grieve even before the baby dies. This "anticipatory
grief" can begin during early signs of miscarriage, premature labor or
emergency cesarean, or when the baby is diagnosed as having a severe
illness or abnormalities. Even as you hope for the best and maybe even
deny the possibility of death, some anticipatory grieving allows you to
prepare yourself. It can also give you the opportunity to say special
goodbyes. When the baby dies, you may feel relieved that the uncertainty
is over. You may also feel relieved that your baby's ordeal has ended. If
the death is sudden and unexpected but due to a disabling condition,
you may feel relief that your baby did not suffer any longer.

Although you may feel relief, you can still expect to feel angry and
sad. Even with anticipatory grieving, your emotions may intensify
after your baby dies.

It wasn't until after she was stillborn that the doctors
discovered she had a fatal heart defect. Although I'm
really angry that something was wrong with her heart,
and that they couldn't know it or do anything about it,
I'm so thankful that she didn't have to suffer.

—Stephanie

## IS IT NORMAL TO FIND COMFORT
## IN NURTURING BEHAVIORS?

Some parents become concerned when they find themselves or their
partner cradling a pillow as if it were a baby or cuddling their baby's
clothes. While these behaviors may seem strange to outsiders, you
may find great comfort in these nurturing gestures. You may want to
consider keeping your baby's nursery intact for a while so you can
spend time holding and caressing your baby's things. You may be
comforted by:

- smelling your baby's clothing
- putting your baby's photograph under your pillow
- sleeping with your baby's pajamas or a teddy bear meant for the baby
- dressing a doll in infant's clothing
- sitting in a rocking chair, cuddling a baby-sized stuffed animal
- writing your baby a loving note in your journal before starting the day or going to sleep at night

Even though the baby is dead, the nurturing instinct can be very strong. By engaging in these behaviors, you can gradually adjust to your baby's absence. It is normal to find comfort in anything that helps you feel close to your baby as you slowly let go. Do what you need to do to cope with your loss.

> The first time we went away for a weekend, I felt like I was abandoning Jamie. So I held the urn that holds her ashes and I wrote a little note to her, telling her how much I loved her and that we'd be back, and I put it on the dresser with her urn.
>
> —Stephanie

## IS IT NORMAL TO ALSO GRIEVE PAST LOSSES?

Besides the secondary losses associated with the death of your baby—the dreams, fantasies, plans for the future—you may be reminded of other losses you've experienced. If other loved ones have died, you may resume any unfinished mourning. If you've lost other children, you may feel that the death of this baby pushes you to the limits of your endurance. The death of your baby can act as a catalyst for you to deal with old, buried emotions and incomplete goodbyes.

In dealing with these old emotions, it helps to pinpoint other losses—and not just those involving death. Human experience contains many different kinds of loss, all warranting some degree of grief. We lose relationships through misunderstandings, shifting interests, moving to distant towns, divorces (particularly our own or our parents'), graduations, changing jobs. Even after we marry and start a family, some friendships fade. These life changes can also involve loss of trust, status, opportunities, goals, familiar places or favorite activities.

Symbolic losses deserve recognition too. For instance, if we lose our great-grandmother's jewelry in a fire, in a burglary or by accident, we may feel as though we've also lost a part of our heritage or the last tangible part of her. Even losses we experienced long ago can be dredged up, such as being dethroned as the only or youngest child when a new sibling arrived or losing confidence or dignity when we had to wear eyeglasses and braces in sixth grade. We may never have acknowledged these previous losses, nor taken the time to deal with our grief over them.

When an overwhelming loss occurs, such as the death of a baby, it is normal for these earlier traumas to rear up and cause despair. Rather than trying to focus solely on your grief over your baby, give yourself permission to acknowledge your feelings about other losses as well. By working through these unfinished mournings, you enhance your ability to cope with your baby's death.

### IS IT NORMAL TO FEEL SO IRRITABLE?

Irritability arises from the fact that you are under a tremendous amount of stress. It isn't easy to cope with the minor inconveniences, delays and aggravations that occur every day. You may notice that you have less patience for things that never bothered you before. Careless drivers or delays in the grocery store checkout line may bring you to the brink of violence. Your partner or other children may drive you to distraction. If something unplanned happens or if you cannot find something you need, you may feel very frustrated. It isn't so easy anymore to shrug off these common inconveniences.

Your intense reactions may be coming from your anger about your baby's death as well as from the stress of grieving. You react with anger because that's the emotion seething under your skin. As time goes on and you work through your grief, you will feel less stressed and less angry, and your patience will return. In the meantime, reduce stress by not making many commitments. For now, grieving over your baby's death and adjusting to your loss are your priorities. Do things that relax you—take a bubble bath, listen to music, take a brisk walk. Find constructive ways to express your anger. (See chapter 6 for ways to cope with anger.) It may help to remind yourself (and others!) that you are having a hard time because your baby died. Sometimes, just knowing where strong reactions are coming from can help you express and work through those feelings.

My reactions were so strong that it was the closest thing
to being insane. I'm a pretty emotional person anyway,
but I don't think I've ever felt that intensely.

—Liza

About four months after Casey died I found myself
turning around once—and I don't even know what it was,
or why—and slapping my youngest child. Then I just fell
to pieces, and I thought, "Oh my gosh, you can't even
control yourself."

—Meryl

### IS IT NORMAL TO FEEL HAPPY SOMETIMES?

At first many bereaved parents feel awkward if they laugh at
something funny or enjoy a pleasurable activity. After all, the baby
is dead. How can anything seem funny or enjoyable in the midst of
such tragedy? If you aren't sad all the time, you may feel disloyal to
the baby, as though you are desecrating the baby's life and death.

To the contrary, it is normal, even healthy, to experience positive
as well as negative emotions while you are in mourning. You deserve
to have respite from the pain and still enjoy the good things life has
to offer.

One time I found myself whistling at work and I couldn't
believe it, you know, that I'd forget for just a little while
and I'd be happy. And then I'd feel guilty that I actually
forgot about the baby.

—Kent

I remember the first time I laughed at something. It really
hit me that I shouldn't be happy about anything, that it
was wrong or disrespectful or something. But then again
it was such a relief to know that I wasn't going to be this
totally somber person for the rest of my life.

—Courtney

### IS IT NORMAL TO FEEL SO ISOLATED?

Many people are unacquainted with miscarriage, stillbirth or infant
death until it happens to them. It is easy to feel alone and isolated

when you are unaware of how often other families are struck by these losses. Unfortunately, this isolation can add to feelings of self-blame and doubt.

> When you feel that you're the only one, your mind can really convince you that it is directly related to your behavior, and you become paranoid. It took me so long to drop the intense guilt and questioning—"What did I do? Was I so sinful? Was this a punishment?"—on and on. When you see that it does happen to all kinds of people— through reading, seeing it on TV, joining a support group—it lessens the questioning and paranoia and helps you do the job of grieving for your child.
>
> —Rose

It is easy to become isolated from friends and family. After the first weeks or months following your baby's death, you may notice that the initial rush of support from others subsides. People seem to expect you to be back to normal and may even say things like "Aren't you over this yet?" or "Buck up—no use crying over spilt milk!" Because you are still grieving so intensely, these remarks can make you wonder if your feelings are silly or unjustified.

Ironically, as the first few months pass, your numbness wears off and you really start grappling with difficult feelings, such as anger and despair. Many mothers report that the third or fourth month is most difficult, and yet people aren't as supportive when they need it most. You may feel that you are grieving alone, that no one else misses your baby the way you do, that no one cares but you.

Try to surround yourself with people who can listen and care. Learn to avoid the insensitive ones. A bereaved parents support group can be a good place to meet people who will help you through your grief, as you in turn help them. Befriending other parents who have experienced this tragic loss can reduce your feelings of isolation. (See chapter 9 for more on support.)

Unfortunately, you will find yourself in situations where people just don't understand what you are going through. This can feel intolerably lonely.

I went right back to work and got involved in that. I thought
I had to put on this big front that everything was fine. So I
was functioning and everybody expected things of me and
people were real sweet, but they didn't know that inside I was
going crazy. I just remember not caring and being frustrated
and just feeling like I was one big act and that inside I was
dying. During the holidays, Thanksgiving was unbearable,
Christmas was unbearable, everything was unbearable.

—Holly

*IS IT NORMAL TO FEEL SO IMPATIENT ABOUT GRIEVING?*
Grieving can be a long, often discouraging process. During the first
several months you may feel that your baby's death will always be the
center of your attention, that nothing positive will ever be realized,
that you will never accept it or integrate it into your life, that you will
never adjust or get back to normal. Other bereaved parents will try
to reassure you that in time you will feel better, but when you are in
such agony, that's hard to believe. Especially after a few months,
when the shock has worn off and you are facing the stark, painful
reality of your baby's death, you may feel more despondent than ever.

Even as you start feeling better, you may experience times when
you feel worse. These setbacks are a normal part of the rollercoaster
of grief, but you may feel very frustrated and discouraged that you
can still feel so terrible. Courtney observes, "Time seems to be
dragging, taking forever! The bad days are as bad as ever, less
frequent but just as bad—like it happened yesterday, so fresh! I just
try to get through one day at a time, although some days I feel like I'm
just trying to get through one minute at a time."

As time goes on, these setbacks happen less frequently and,
eventually, are less overwhelming. In hindsight, many parents can see
that the passage of time is a healing thing.

I remember feeling impatient because I wanted my
emotions and my heart to heal as quickly as my abdomen.
I knew that wasn't going to happen, but the feeling was "I
want to be done crying, I want to be done being sad, I
want to be done being angry, I just want to wrap this up
and get on with my life."

—Sophie

It's a very sad thing, but you don't feel like such a victim
after you get to a certain point. You just go on, and time
will finally just do something that does kind of help."

—Bryn

Time is a very good healer. I think for everything that
happens to me, if I can just take a breath and think,
"Someday I'm going to see this from a different perspective," I think it helps me get through.

—Jane

## IS IT NORMAL TO FEEL SUICIDAL?

At some point, many mothers feel it would be easier to end it all than
to cope with their baby's death and the turmoil of grief. Some
thoughts of suicide are harmless, while others can be quite serious,
leading to an actual suicide attempt. Basically, there are two kinds of
suicidal feelings: passive and active. Passive feelings occur when you
think about suicide as an option but don't make plans to actually do
it. These passive thoughts of suicide are like fantasies—you comfort
yourself by imagining death as an escape from despair or as a way to
be reunited with your baby.

Active feelings are evident when you make concrete plans for
committing suicide. You may buy an overdose of sleeping pills or
devise plans to drive over a cliff. Rose recalls, "I knew exactly where
the gun was and I was wondering how I could do it where I would be
sure that I would die and not be a vegetable. Then I would think, 'No,
I can't do that. I would really hurt a lot of people.' And then I'd think,
'No, I wouldn't, they would just go on with their lives just like after
Jessica died.' "

If you are concerned about your suicidal feelings, talk to a friend,
your partner or one of the following resources:

- your doctor
- a suicide hotline (look under Emergency Numbers often
  listed inside the front cover of the phone book)
- a community mental health agency (look for a 24-hour
  or "crisis" number under Hospitals or Mental Health
  Services in the Yellow Pages)

Talking about your feelings with someone who cares can help you see other ways to function, other options for coping. With or without help, it can be a struggle to keep a perspective on things. Maria remembers: "I had a really bad night and I thought about overdosing on Valium, but then I thought about my husband and my 2 year old, and I couldn't do that to them."

> I remember that first week, waking up one night shaking and losing control. I told my husband, "I want to die, I just want to die, and I want to be with my baby and if that's what it takes, then I want to die, God just take me, please!" I couldn't take my own life, but if it happened, it would have been welcomed because I would have been with Nicole. I kept thinking, "Why didn't I die too, why didn't we both die together? And then we'd be together." At that time, Nicole was the only important thing in my life. I couldn't see ahead, I couldn't think ahead. All I thought was, "I want my baby and if that's what it takes, let it be."
>
> —Cindy

### IS IT NORMAL TO THINK ABOUT YOUR BABY SO OFTEN?

There may be times when your thoughts are consumed by your baby: you hear cries, you see something that makes you think he or she is alive and well, or you vividly dream about your baby. You may have trouble concentrating or remembering things because you feel so preoccupied.

These illusions and thoughts are not abnormal or morbid. Going over your memories, hopes and dreams is a central part of the grieving process. You can also benefit by telling your story over and over to friends and acquaintances. This is your mind's way of gradually adjusting to the fact that your baby is dead and your plans have changed. For instance, you may have envisioned sharing certain times of the year with your new baby—taking your baby to the beach during the summer or visiting your parents at Thanksgiving, baby in tow. Maybe you resent going back to work sooner than you had originally planned because you thought you would be staying home with the baby. Part of grieving over your baby's death is recognizing that you lost more than just your baby—you lost all your plans for parenthood and your dreams for this baby. Repeatedly thinking about all these losses and changes is the way you gradually adjust to them.

Parents vary in how often they think about their baby. At first you may feel preoccupied with the circumstances surrounding your baby's life and death—whether your baby died early in your pregnancy or many months after birth. As time passes and you adjust to your loss, you will gradually feel less preoccupied with your baby and you'll regain interest in your regular activities. Even months later, however, some mothers report thinking about their babies many times a day or several times a week.

More important than how often you think about your baby is whether thinking about your baby prevents you from getting things accomplished. At first, this will be the case, but eventually you'll discover that you can think about the baby without dissolving into tears. If you stumble into the baby food aisle in the grocery store, you may think wistfully about what might have been, but you can still finish the shopping. If a colleague brings baby pictures to work, you can be reminded of your own baby and still finish the task at hand.

As the years pass, mothers who think daily about their baby point out that it can become a ritual rather than an obsession. Some mothers include their baby in nightly prayers or have a picture or other memento displayed in a special place.

> It's kind of hard to describe, but I just thought about
> Laura all the time, just constantly. In the first few weeks I
> could probably think of maybe half an hour where I
> didn't think of her, when I was distracted. But it was just
> a real constant dwelling on her and talking about her and
> what had happened. Then it lessened and I was aware of
> thinking about her several times a day. But I thought
> about her an awful lot for an awfully long time—for at
> least a year, intensely for at least six months.
>
> —Hannah

## IS IT NORMAL TO FEEL YOUR BABY'S PRESENCE?

Many mothers report feeling their baby's presence. You may have spiritual beliefs that your baby exists in heaven or on another plane and that perhaps you will be reunited upon your own death. These beliefs can give you great comfort.

> One evening I heard three slow knocks on the front door.
> I had a feeling no one would be there, but I opened the
> door anyway and I felt a rush of warm air. Was that
> Matthew?
>
> —Kea

> I believe in an afterlife, so I don't believe Jessica is com-
> pletely out of my life. I don't believe she's hovering
> around or anything, but I believe she is somewhere, in a
> place, and eventually, someday, when I die that I'll be in
> the same place.
>
> —Rose

## IS IT NORMAL TO FEEL LIKE A CHANGED PERSON?

> I don't particularly think everything's going to go uphill
> all the time anymore. I don't count on things. I can't be
> quite as trusting as I maybe was before.
>
> —Hannah

Bereaved parents often remark that they feel changed. At first, while you grieve intensely, you may feel more temperamental, more pessimistic and more sensitive than usual. But as you work through your grief, you will notice that it is more your perspective than your personality that changes. You may feel older, wiser, more vulnerable to tragedy, more a part of the cycle of life and death. Like many mothers, Anya observes, "I've learned more about myself, that I'm stronger than I thought I was." You may feel that certain things such as work, money, status and expensive possessions have lost some of their value. You may find a heightened appreciation for other things, including children, fertility, health, life, supportive relationships and yourself.

> When Jessica died, everything lost meaning. I just don't
> care about anything except spiritual things, eternal things,
> things that last. Relationships are much more important

to me, deep relationships. My only long-term goal is raising my kids. Since Jessica died, being a mother means everything.

—Rose

I feel like my values are different. A big nice house isn't important to me anymore. It's more simple things, like spending time with my husband.

—Kelly

## SHOULD I FEEL BETTER AFTER A CERTAIN PERIOD OF TIME?

Throw deadlines out the window. Don't place expectations on yourself to feel better after a certain amount of time. Give yourself permission to feel your feelings, to feel bad when you feel bad and to start to feel better whenever that occurs. Remember that grief has its ups and downs, and you will feel discouraged when you have setbacks. You deserve all the time you need. Do what is best for you, what you need to do to cope with your baby's death.

It's been nearly two years since Kevin died, and I'm having a hard time these days. I think I should be feeling better than this! Kevin would have been two years old this month. My baby daughter is now the age Kevin was when he died. It's the holiday season, and I should have three children, not just two. After my new baby was born, I grieved very hard. But after a few weeks I thought, "That's enough, I'm done," and I put Kevin's photo album away. But I guess I need to give myself permission to grieve some more, as long as I need to.

—Cathryn

## POINTS TO REMEMBER

- It is normal to feel bad about tough, painful decisions you had to make; feeling bad does not mean you made a bad decision.
- It is normal to feel crazy; grief is a bewildering experience.
- It is normal to feel relief; anticipatory grieving can give you the opportunity to prepare yourself for your baby's death.
- It is normal to find comfort in nurturing behaviors; do things that let you remember and feel close to your baby.
- It is normal to grieve for past losses; acknowledging these bereavements can enhance your ability to cope with your baby's death.
- It is normal to be irritable; try to reduce your stress by finding constructive outlets for your anger as well as engaging in relaxing activities.
- It is normal to be happy sometimes; enjoy any respite from your grief.
- It is normal to feel isolated; surround yourself with people who care.
- It is normal to feel impatient with grief; let yourself have bad days.
- It is normal to feel suicidal; fantasizing about reunion with your baby can help you cope, but get help if you are concerned or make concrete suicide plans.
- It is normal to think about the baby often; going over memories of your baby and what might have been can help you gradually adjust to your loss.
- It is normal to feel the baby's presence; find comfort in the belief that your baby exists somewhere else.
- It is normal to feel like a changed person; many parents grow emotionally as a result of experience with loss and grief.
- It is normal to expect to feel better after a certain deadline, but allow yourself the time to grieve without regard to how many months or years have passed.

# 5

# Affirming Your Baby

## MEMORIES AND GRIEF

Memories can help you cope with your grief. Although it can be painful, dwelling on memories is a way for you to slowly adjust to your baby's absence. Memories allow you to reminisce about your pregnancy or the baby's special qualities and happier times. Memories make it possible for you to say goodbye to your baby at a gradual pace. If friends and relatives also had a chance to know this baby, their memories enable them to recognize the significance of your loss and to share your grief more easily.

When the time you spent with your baby was cut short, whether due to miscarriage, stillbirth or infant death, there are few memories to hold on to or share with others. This makes grieving difficult, whether you are able to recall a little person or simply a person who might have been. You may have difficulty acknowledging your grief because it is not so clear how this baby fit into your life, nor did you have much opportunity to become acquainted. The baby is gone, leaving little tangible evidence of his or her existence. Even if your baby lived for many months, you may feel an intense emptiness as you grieve the loss of the hopes, wishes and fantasies associated with this child and the future. You may idealize the baby and resist letting go. ("Maybe this was just the child we wanted.") You may feel isolated in your grief, having no one to share memories and swap stories with. Some friends and family members may fail to recognize this baby's special significance, making you feel as though your grief is invalid. Most notably, grieving can be painfully difficult because the lack of memories makes your adjustment seem overwhelming and goodbyes too abrupt.

In the past, mothers were encouraged to forget their dead babies. Because there was so little to remember, it was assumed to be an easy task. However, it is not so easy, because to forget is to abandon a part of yourself. You need help in remembering and affirming your baby so you will be better able to grieve and adjust to a different future. When your baby dies, you benefit from getting to know the baby and gathering as many memories as possible.

> A lot of people say, "It would've been worse if she had lived." But I think if I had even one hour with my child alive, thank God for that hour. I feel cheated. ... I didn't have any time with her outside of my body. I thought, "If you just give me fifteen minutes, just a little bit of time—just to tell her that I love her and to know that she heard me and to know that she knew, that she was alive and breathing when I told her that." So I don't like people to tell me that it would've been worse.
>
> —Cindy

> A friend of mine lost a baby when he was 6 months old, and she was saying, "You just don't know how lucky you are that your baby was taken at birth." I said, "At least you have some memories!" I really *wanted* to have some memories.
>
> —Bryn

## EVERY BABY IS IMPORTANT

When your baby was miscarried, was stillborn or died shortly after birth, you need to affirm your baby's life however possible—by gathering mementos such as ultrasound pictures or photographs, sorting through your baby's things or having opportunities to hold the baby. Visiting the grave site or the place where you keep the ashes also commemorates your baby's existence.

After your baby dies, you also need to affirm your baby's importance and the significance of your loss. To do this you may want to arrange rituals and create memorials that acknowledge your baby's life. By arranging funeral or memorial services or by sending out announcements, you are inviting family and friends to recognize this devastating loss, giving them a chance to realize your baby's importance and to grieve along with you. These rituals also provide you with more memories of your baby. Creating memorials can help you honor your baby's place in your life.

Sadly, some opportunities for making memories and collecting mementos may have already passed. It may be too late to take photographs, clip a wisp of hair or dress the baby. In retrospect you may wish you had decided on burial instead of hospital cremation. How could you have known at the time that these would be comforting things to do? These circumstances must be grieved also. Expressing anger, disappointment and sorrow at these losses can help you cope with them.

> At this hospital they didn't take pictures, they didn't save anything, they didn't do anything. I didn't realize at the time that you need all these things. I didn't know that the mementos would be important, that the picture would be all-important and that holding the baby is real important for the grieving process. ... That's probably, above all, the thing that makes me the angriest or the saddest. It's like, if she *had* to die, they could've *at least* handled it right!
>
> —Holly

> Kevin was our second child, and you know how it is with the second one. In the three months he was with us, I only took enough pictures to fill three pages in the photo album. I never clipped a wisp of his hair. I feel so bad about that. I wish I had more things to remember him by.
>
> —Cathryn

Even though you may have some regrets about decisions made or circumstances that may have been out of your control, there are still some things you can do. It's never too late to remember and memorialize your baby in special ways.

## REMEMBERING YOUR BABY

### MEMORIES OF YOUR PREGNANCY

Your pregnancy holds a major chunk of memories of this baby. These memories can be especially important if you suffered a miscarriage.

You may recollect the day you discovered you were pregnant, the excitement of hearing the fetal heartbeat or the first time you saw your baby's image on an ultrasound screen. If you carried your baby well into the second trimester, you may be able to remember the first time you felt your baby move inside you. Was this a quiet or a rambunctious baby? Did he get the hiccups often? Did she like to stretch out? You may want to set aside a few maternity outfits that you especially associate with this time, instead of giving them away. Your "positive" pregnancy test slip or any ultrasound pictures may also be cherished as mementos.

If you delivered in the hospital, you may find it helpful to go over the events of labor and delivery with your doctor and nurses, especially if you were medicated. Details about the baby's birth, illness and condition are additional memories to recall during your grieving process.

If you have unanswered questions about your baby, even if it is years later, you can request medical records from the hospital. The more you know, the more you can resolve your grief.

> I went back later to the hospital and met my primary
> nurse because I wanted to know everything that had
> happened. She answered all my questions and told me
> everything my mind couldn't fill in. She told me what the
> baby looked like, which was really sweet because that's
> really all I have, is what she told me.
>
> —Holly

> When my second baby died at 18 weeks, they didn't let
> me see it. They wouldn't even tell me if it was a boy or a
> girl. The doctor just said, "You don't need to know that."
> So now, seven years later, after my baby girl Susan was
> stillborn, it brought back a lot of questions about my
> other baby. With the encouragement of my parent
> support group, I went back to that hospital and requested
> the medical records to get some answers. The baby was a
> little boy—I named him David—and now I feel like I have
> a better idea about what I lost, who I grieve for.
>
> —Janet

## MEMORIES OF BEING WITH YOUR BABY

As you grieve, you can reflect on memories of being with your baby. During your pregnancy, your baby was cradled inside you. If you were able to hold your baby after delivery, you can try to remember how he or she looked and felt. If your baby lived many days or months after birth, you had more opportunities to get to know your baby. Although it may never seem like enough, these memories can be cherished.

I remember when they brought David in. My husband was standing there at the bed and I was laying in the bed and the nurse walked in the door with the baby all wrapped up as a newborn, and I remember thinking in that short distance from the door to me, "What was she going to do? Was she going to put him in my arms? Was she going to lay him on the bed? What was she going to do?" And very naturally she walked in, didn't say a word and handed me the baby and left. We immediately started to cry very, very hard, and I took his little hand and held it around my finger the way you do any baby and I just held him like that and kept looking at him ... and then my husband leaned down and kissed him on the forehead.

—Bess

I spent most of the afternoon holding her, and then they withdrew life-support systems, disconnected everything, and we held her again. It was so sad, but I'm really glad we were able to hold her as much as we did. I think maybe it helped her a little bit, at least she had us there to hold her.

—Hannah

Right before they took Stephanie off the machines, we each had hold of one of her hands. ... Then she opened her eyes and she was gripping each of our hands, which was amazing because she was so sick. It was like she was acknowledging we were there. It was as though she was saying, "It's OK, I love you and I know you love me and I'm leaving." It was amazing we had that same sense, that message from her.

—Sophie

Memories of being with your baby are important because they confirm the fact that a baby really existed. If you were able to see your baby, this experience helps you view the baby as an individual and gives you someone tangible to mourn. Holding and touching your baby also gave you an opportunity to express your love in a physical way. Being with your baby before and after death gave you an opportunity to say hello *and* goodbye.

> He was *so little* . ... I knew there was no way he could live, he was just too little. As they were wheeling him by they let me hug him, and I told him his name and I told him how much I loved him ... because I knew I wouldn't have much chance to do that.
>
> —Lena

> I was only 12 weeks along, and being able to see the tiny baby helped. She fit right in the palm of my hand. ... I wasn't sure what to wrap her in for the trip to the hospital, and then I thought of my grandmother's lace handkerchiefs. So I picked one out and wrapped her up very carefully.
>
> —Clara

> I think when I was going through nursing school, the attitude was more "Just don't let the mother see the baby." And that's the opposite of what you really need. Holding her was good because we knew her from during the pregnancy, and now here she was and she was a real baby and a real person. That helped, rather than just "she's gone, there's nothing to it, just like it didn't happen, you didn't have that baby inside you for nine months and just forget about it. ..." There really was a baby there.
>
> —Hannah

Seeing the baby after delivery also alleviates fears about the baby being horribly deformed. Fantasies are usually much worse than reality, and parents are often relieved at how normal and beautiful the baby looks. Even if the baby is malformed, health-care professionals have noticed that parents focus on and find comfort in positive body features. Seeing the baby also satisfies curiosity about what the baby looks like and can help parents register and verify the fact that the baby is dead.

If your baby died before or shortly after birth, some people will wonder if holding your baby makes grief more painful because you risk becoming too attached. You can remind them that you've already held the baby in your womb and felt a bond long before your baby died.

> I was glad I held the baby. It helped a lot to be able to see him and hold him and know that they didn't take our baby and give it to someone else and give us a dead baby. It helped to know that he was ours.
>
> —Martina

> If I hadn't seen her, definitely her—with the hospital band that said Jessica—dead, I don't think I could've settled it in my mind that she was really dead.
>
> —Rose

> After he was born they brought him up to the bed, and my husband and I sat and looked at him and touched him. I was glad. That was really the best thing that could've happened. I think I thought he was probably a monster, that he was deformed, that there was something wrong with him. He was a beautiful baby. I think it also helped to ease the sorrow and filled in all those empty areas where I could have wondered what he looked like or what he would have been. Just seeing him gave him a personality, a real concrete substance.
>
> —Meryl

If you were not encouraged or allowed to see your baby, you may feel angry or cheated or desperately curious about your baby's appearance. You may feel an added sense of loss that not only is your baby dead, but you were denied the only chance you had to hold him or her. If you had a miscarriage, you may not have known what to look for, or your doctor may not have allowed you to see the baby or the remains after a D & C. Being able to see whatever there was might have been helpful.

Although researchers have found that most parents regret not seeing their baby, there are some parents who fear that seeing the baby would be too upsetting. They want to remember the baby as they imagined during pregnancy. Fortunately, hospital policies are changing. Most healthcare providers recognize how important it is to encourage parents to hold their baby, but realize the choice is a personal one.

With miscarriage and D & C, changes are coming about more slowly. If you wish you could have seen your baby's remains, inform your doctor. This choice may then be offered to others.

> The doctor wouldn't tell me anything about Matthew. He just said, "The baby was normal. That's all you need to know." But I've had nightmares about him, what he is like in the grave, digging him up, things like that. I still wonder what he looked like. Every once in a while I think about what's happening in the grave, and I don't know why I do that. I guess I just wonder what it would be like to look at him now. I think I'm just obsessed. I needed to see him.
>
> —Desi

### NEVER ENOUGH TIME

Parents who are able to see their baby are generally glad to have that experience. However, they also report regrets, such as not having more time with the baby or not doing nurturing things such as cuddling or dressing their baby's body. Although it can be painful, it is necessary to grieve for these missed opportunities. You can cope more easily if you pinpoint these moments and talk or write about your thoughts and feelings instead of burying them and letting them fester. (See chapter 6 on coping with anger and guilt.)

It is also helpful to know that you are not alone. Many parents express regret that they were unable to spend more time with their baby before death. If the baby was placed in intensive care or transported to another hospital for treatment, this sense is heightened. Rose's baby was transported to a children's hospital after delivery, but they didn't run any tests for two days. She says, "I'm really angry about that. ... If she was just laying there, she could've been laying there with me. I just remember there was no concern about me being with the baby. Of course, at the time I thought I'd have a lifetime with her so I wasn't that concerned."

Stephanie wishes she could have seen the color of her daughter's eyes or felt the grip of her tiny hand. This is a common regret of mothers who have suffered miscarriage or stillbirth. Many parents feel they were not given enough time to spend with the baby or that they felt confused, rushed or morbid, so they gave up the baby before they were ready. Kelly points out, "I really resent not being awake for Scott's delivery. I can accept his death a lot better than I can accept not being with him for the few hours he was alive." Many, like Kara and Liza, didn't realize or couldn't grasp how seriously ill their baby was.

When Matthew was born they handed him to me and said, "Oh, this looks like a healthy little baby boy." He was beautiful. But the nurse picked him up right away because he was having trouble. So that was the only time that I got to hold him while he was alive and it just seemed like it was only a second. Looking back on it now, I wish I could've held him a little longer, but I just didn't see the tragedy that was going to occur. When he was in intensive care, we kept vigil as much as we could. I was right on top of him, as close as I could be to him. Then, after he died, I demanded that we see him. It was like, "You're not taking my baby. I want to see him RIGHT NOW." Nowadays, I wish I could have held him much, much more before and after he died.

—Kara

I've always wished it were longer. But it felt like I was supposed to give him to the doctor, like he was going to take Daniel back over and put him on the oxygen. It was like he's not really dying, this is some kind of game or something. But I always wonder why I didn't hold him longer—there was so much confusion.

—Liza

Looking back, many mothers wish that the nurses had offered the baby again, more than once or twice. Mothers need time to recover from shock or from anesthesia so they can spend a more meaningful time with the baby. Seeing the baby again also helps parents remember more. Bryn and Holly talk about their disappointing experiences:

> I still feel kind of cheated because I was in such a state of shock. I remember looking at the baby, but I cannot remember what he looked like. I remember asking the doctor to go ahead and take him away because I was afraid I was going to get crazy and say, "No, you can't have my baby." I don't think I would have, but you just don't know what you're doing. I wish they had offered him to us again later.
>
> —Bryn

> After I came out of the anesthesia I was really out of it, but the doctor brought her into the recovery room. ... I held her and touched her but I couldn't really move or anything because I was in such pain. One of the things that's real frustrating to me is I can't remember her because I was so out of it.
>
> —Holly

If a baby dies before or shortly after birth, it may not occur to the parents to unwrap their baby and caress the little body or dress the baby in special clothing. As Erin says, "It would've helped me to be able to dress her, so she could've felt my touch somehow ... ." Some parents wish they'd had more privacy so that they could have felt free to explore their baby's body or express emotions without feeling self-conscious. Kara recalls, "There were people there and it was great having their support, but I just kept feeling interrupted."

Parents who are able to see their baby later may be dismayed when the baby is cold. Cindy wishes the nurses had warmed her baby so that holding and touching her would have been more comforting. She remembers, "I held her again the next morning and she was like a block of ice. I could almost not hold her. I kissed her forehead and it was so cold."

Later, many parents wish that others in their family and circle of friends could have seen the baby, so that these people could have gotten to know the baby too. The parents' other children might have also benefited from seeing the baby.

Some parents regret giving in to pressure from a partner or other relatives to not see the baby or to cut the visit short. Lena, Rose and Kara had husbands or other relatives who were trying to protect them from their sadness instead of letting them face it.

> Life support was taken off him, and we let him go for it. Looking back on it, I wish I had held him as he died. But at the time, I think my husband was trying to protect me because he knew how much I wanted that baby. So when he approached me about it, he said, "You don't want to hold him now do you?" and I went, "No." ... I deferred to his judgment. I was a little mouse. Looking back on it, I wish that I had cuddled Stephen close. If I had to do it over again, I would pick him up and hold him, hug him, rock him, talk to him and sing to him. Hugging him in his incubator isn't quite the same.
>
> —Lena

> My husband felt like I needed to rest, so I remember he took me home. I was fighting and screaming all the way. I didn't want to go. I just wanted to spend the time with the baby. This was the first day I'd had with her and he was just *so* insistent and at the time I just wasn't as confident. I wasn't the kind of person who would say, "I'm staying. You can go home if you want to." I wasn't that person then. I was a lot younger, dumber, less confident. So now I have all these things I should have done, to spend any second that I had with her.
>
> —Rose

> My mother-in-law was saying, "Well, you know, you need to let go. The longer you hold on to him, the harder it is to give him up." And I was kind of, "Well, maybe she's right." But I could've held on to him longer. I wanted to hold on to him longer.
>
> —Kara

In hindsight, you may wonder why you didn't demand more time with the baby or do more things like kissing and cuddling. But you did the best you could at the time. Even mothers who feel like they spent plenty of time with the baby will always wish they could have had more time, a lifetime with the baby.

## PHOTOGRAPHS

Photographs can be some of your most treasured mementos. Particularly if you experienced an early miscarriage, any pictures of you during that pregnancy can be special. If your baby never left the hospital, photographs may have been taken by a healthcare provider and offered to you. Or you may have been able to use your own camera. (Polaroid photos fade over time, but you can take them to a custom film developing lab and ask for a copy negative, which will last.) If your baby was at home, you may have many photographs to keep. Having at least one good quality photograph can help you remember your baby. Along with other mementos, it helps acknowledge the baby's existence and your loss in a tangible way.

> I'm really glad we have pictures. I look at them a lot. Some people think that they're kind of gruesome, but they're real important to me.
>
> —Jessie

> I'm glad we've got a picture because you never forget the baby but you can forget how they look, and later on if you want to look at it, you can.
>
> —Martina

> When they asked if we wanted them to take some pictures of him, at the time I thought, "You've got to be kidding me. That's disgusting!" And a week or so later someone from the hospital called and said, "I've got these photographs of Matthew and I'd really like to send them to you." I said, "Send them! I want them!" Now we treasure them. The pictures are something that really helps me go through the grieving process.
>
> —Kara

If you don't have a picture of your baby, you may feel a lack of tangible evidence that your baby existed. Some parents find it helpful to have a picture to show to friends and relatives, or to their other children so they could see their brother or sister. Bryn wishes she had a picture to refresh her memory because she can't remember her baby's face. This is difficult for her "because he was a part of me." For others, like Dara, a photograph would have been their only chance to see what the baby looked like. Dara remembers that the pathology department at her hospital took photographs for research purposes, but they've never been able to get copies. She says, "That's something I go through in phases every once in a while, wanting to try again and get them." Desi was never able to see her baby, nor were photographs taken, but she believes her curiosity could be somewhat satisfied by seeing someone else's picture: "I want mothers in my support group to bring a picture of their dead baby so I can see what they look like. But I never have the nerve to ask anybody."

Parents who do have photographs may be dissatisfied with the quality or wish they had one of the baby before death or of a closeup of the face, the undressed body or them holding their baby. Anya has most of these regrets, but it still helps her to have photographs of Rachel. She notes, "The pictures are blurry and fuzzy and don't look like much, but I know they're there. It's real important. It's something tangible."

If you don't have a photograph or if your photographs are disappointing, you can have a portrait drawn or painted of your baby. One mother took her single blurry photograph to a portrait artist who did a wonderful job of capturing what her baby looked like. Another mother, whose baby died thirteen weeks into the pregnancy, took a collection of family baby pictures to an artist who drew a portrait of what the baby might have looked like as an infant. You can also collect other pictures that hold meaning—of places, things or people you associate with the baby.

Photographs and portraits are one way of preserving a memory, but not the only way. If you don't have a portrait of your baby, you can still imagine what he or she looked like and hold that picture in your mind's eye.

## KEEPSAKES
Mementos of the baby that you may treasure include footprints, record of the baby's length and weight, lock of hair, hospital ID

bracelet, autopsy report, sympathy cards and flowers, any clothing or toys or stuffed animals you acquired, and baptismal, birth and death certificates. You may collect recordings of special songs you associate with your baby or your pregnancy. Even if you were pregnant for a short time, you can save anything you associate with this time period. Some parents keep these mementos in a special box, baby book or envelope and look through them as a way to spend time with and affirm their baby. Even if these keepsakes are tucked away in a drawer, it helps to know you have them.

> I kept all the flowers. I have them dried in a little glass vase with a cork in it. It means a lot to me. I still have the ribbons from the graveside service. That really helps to keep things like that.
>
> —Rayleen

> I love my mementos. It's good for me, another thing that makes it real. I have a picture of my baby; I have her hair. She was alive at one time and she was my daughter, and you just can't pretend she isn't real. So it does, it makes it real.
>
> —Cindy

If your baby died before birth, you will not receive an official birth certificate. This can feel disappointing because it somehow denies the fact that your baby was alive inside you! As an alternative, some hospitals provide a "baby certificate," which lists the baby's name, date of birth and other life affirming information. You can also design your own certificate or find a print shop to make one for you.

Often when a baby dies, people assume that baby gifts would be meaningless or painful to the parents. To the contrary, these gifts can be viewed as acknowledgments of your baby and can serve as treasured mementos. If someone mentions it or if you know a gift was being made for your baby, don't hesitate to tell them how meaningful it would be.

If you feel pressure to go through your baby's things and put away the nursery, wait until you are ready. Putting baby things away is a big step in saying goodbye, and you may need more time. Meanwhile, it may help just to spend time in your baby's room, among your baby's things.

I remember I would take Matthew's little cap he wore in
the incubator and smell it after he died because I can
remember that it smelled like him. ... I saved everything I
could. He was real important to us.

—Kara

# RITUALS

*A NAME FOR YOUR BABY*
Naming the baby is another way to acknowledge the baby's existence
and individuality. A name is personal and lasting. If you suffered a
miscarriage or stillbirth, you may wonder if a name is appropriate.
Do whatever feels right to you. Some parents may want to save a
favorite name for a future baby. Others feel that the name originally
chosen rightfully belongs to this baby.

Giving the baby a nickname or other term of endearment may be
most meaningful to you. Some mothers use the Native American
custom of choosing a name associated with nature, Mother Earth or
celestial bodies to encompass their intuitions about the baby's
spiritual essence. Many mothers have remarked how naming their
baby, even years later, assigns a specific identity to the baby and gives
them someone tangible to mourn.

You may name your baby informally or formally, recording the
baby's name on all documents. Later, if you want to officially change
or add to the baby's name, you can contact the state agency that
handles birth and death certificates.

My family decided that we weren't going to name him,
and I can remember coming up out of that hospital bed
and saying, "OH YES WE ARE!"

—Desi

We all talked so much about her and we called her by
name—Melanie. I was happy that people could say her
name so easily.

—Kitty

*RESPECT FOR YOUR BABY'S BODY*
It is natural for you to have protective urges toward your baby, even

after the baby dies. The thought of the baby being cold and alone somewhere in the hospital may seem unbearable. You need your baby's body to be treated with respect—it is a gesture that confirms your baby's importance and worth. If hospital staff are providing you with emotional support, it is also likely that they are treating your baby's body respectfully. For your sake, the baby should be kept comfortable, even after death.

> I remember going back to the hospital, and my nurse friend took me to the room where they had put the baby and then left him there for a little while. That upset me so much, not that they'd done anything wrong, but that he'd been alone. I just kept thinking he was alone in there, the poor thing, and he was cold, and that upset me.
>
> —Bess

### BAPTISM

For some parents, baptism is a meaningful way to have the baby recognized as a valued and real person. For these parents, the baptism holds special memories and a baptismal certificate is another treasured memento. Meryl asked her priest to come to the hospital and bless her baby because she wanted acknowledgment that this baby was a person, that he had lived. She remembers, "Even though he wasn't born alive, he needed that blessing—*I* needed the blessing."

### BURIAL OR CREMATION

If you buried your baby, the grave site can be a place where you can go to be with the baby and express your sadness. If you cremated your baby's body, you may decide to scatter the ashes in a special place that you can visit. Or you may decide to keep the ashes. Many parents find comfort in knowing where the baby's body or ashes lie. If you decide you don't want to keep the ashes forever, it still may take you a long time to feel ready to scatter them or place them in a cemetery. No matter when you are ready, it may help you feel a sense of closure.

> It was important to me for quite some time to have a grave I could visit and to pick out a special bronze plaque that's in granite.
>
> —Anya

I think it helps us to know we have a place to visit and we can see where it says David, Son of ... and I think that's real helpful somehow.

—Bess

Three months after Daniel died, we finally walked to the top of a mountain and let his ashes go. There was a real sense of ... that his spirit was already free and that it was trying to let go.

—Liza

In hindsight you may wonder if you should have done some things differently. Holly wishes they had scattered her baby's ashes in a more accessible spot. Erin wishes she hadn't let the hospital handle her daughter's cremation and burial. She says, "I think if I could do it over again, I would take Barbie's little remains and say something, rites over her, and place her remains in a little tiny coffin box. I just think it would have helped me know that she's OK, she's all in one piece, she's all together. ... Sometimes I just wonder why we didn't do that. When we drive by the cemetery I always think of her. I think she's in there somewhere. I hope she's there."

If you have regrets, express your anger and sorrow about them and then figure out ways to memorialize your baby—ways that hold meaning for you now. Even if you don't know where your baby's remains are, you can have a headstone or plaque made for your baby and put it in a special place. You can put flowers in a peaceful part of a cemetery. Any of these gestures can confirm your love and help you grieve.

## FUNERAL OR MEMORIAL SERVICE

Although it can seem sorrowful, a funeral or memorial service for your baby can be helpful in a number of ways. A service creates an opportunity to say a special goodbye. It acknowledges your loss and need for comfort and support. Friends and family can share your sorrow and, in turn, lessen the isolation you may feel. Any ritualized gestures—naming, baptism, burial, scattering ashes, funeral or memorial service—whether simple or elaborate, can heighten your friends' and relatives' ability to recognize your loss as significant and enable them to give support. With this support, you may feel better able to cope.

Because most parents have not had experience arranging a burial, cremation or memorial service, the process itself may pose too many obstacles. Bess wishes they could have done more than just arrange a private graveside service. Dara feels that it wasn't enough to just dedicate a mass to their baby. Rose had feared that no one cared, but after so many people attended the graveside service, she wished they had arranged a "full-blown funeral in a church." Holly also remembers thinking no one would come and now wonders if it is too late to have some kind of memorial service, just to "add to making it a more real thing, that she had been a *child*."

It is important to remember that memorial services are appropriate any time you feel ready or decide it's something that you want to do. Any rituals that allow you to say goodbye can help. You can arrange a formal memorial service and invite a lot of people, or you can keep it small and private by inviting only a few people or even just your clergyperson. You can read something that has a special meaning as you spread the ashes. Any memorializing gesture like this can be a release—a way of letting go. What's important is that you make arrangements that suit your special needs.

> To do nothing would be to act like she'd never existed. I had a need to acknowledge that she was here ... to make a statement about her being here and what she meant to us. What we didn't anticipate was the response that we got from other people. As a result of both the announcement and the service, people were a terrific support for us. Also, I didn't account for the fact that a lot of those people and some of our close friends had a need to grieve. The service helped them do that as well. It was a good decision.
>
> —Sophie

> In ways I think it would've been good to have a service in order to have closure. But I got that closure when I went up to visit his grave. I realize talking to a stone on the ground is kind of absurd, but I managed to get out a lot of the things I would've said to him if he had lived and I'd had the time to say them. To me that was important.
>
> —Lena

We decided not to have a funeral because Nick and I
knew him and I just couldn't see people coming because
they didn't know him and maybe they wanted to express
their sadness for us, but we didn't feel right about it. ...
To scatter his ashes was a release; it was our letting go.

—Kara

## MEMORIALIZING YOUR BABY

Most parents find it helpful to have the baby memorialized in a
tangible way. There are many ways to publicly acknowledge your
baby's existence. You can have your baby's name engraved in stone
or brass and mounted somewhere meaningful. You can write a poem
or a story about your baby and publish it in a newsletter, magazine
or newspaper. On anniversary dates or holidays you may want to
sponsor flowers at a religious service or make a donation in your
baby's name to a charity or research foundation associated with the
cause of death. During the Christmas season, some philanthropic
organizations give out names of needy children. If it makes you feel
good, buy something for a child that is the age your child would have
been. Donate some helium balloons to a children's hospital or the
intensive care unit where your baby stayed. Jessie and Kent donated
a tree to a botanic garden in Meghan's memory. After Clara's second
miscarriage, she sent announcements to family and friends. This
enabled her to acknowledge her baby and share her grief. The
announcement read, "It is with great sorrow that we inform you of
the passing of our child Emily Rose. We know that you understand
the importance of this child in our life and will share in our grief."
You may think of other meaningful, public ways to honor the
memory of your baby.

There are also many private ways to memorialize your baby. You
may find it comforting to plant a tree or a flowering shrub in your
garden or keep a houseplant as a living memorial to your baby. You
can display the baby's portrait in a special frame somewhere in your
house. During the holiday season—or any time of year—you may
want to display an ornament or burn a candle in memory of your
baby. You could buy a piece of jewelry or another object of some
value that symbolizes your baby; for instance, Courtney wears a
necklace with a gold, heart-shaped locket containing a wisp of her
baby's hair.

You may want to make your own memorials—patchwork, quilting, needlework, knitting, sewing, doll making, drawing, painting, silkscreening, journaling, engraving, sculpting, gardening, flower arranging, stained glass working, pottery, poetry or music. Build a piece of furniture, hang things on a wall, display things under glass or frame anything that reminds you of your baby. Janet made her own memento by designing a card with her baby's name and date of birth and death. She included a poem and Susan's footprints and had it professionally printed and framed. John made a pine chest to hold mementos of Jacob. Eva received a potted plant upon William's death, giving her "something meaningful to nurture."

Many parents find that the creativity involved in these projects gives them a sense of accomplishment and worth—that they are still capable of making beauty after their baby's death.

Some friends gave us a houseplant and I thought, "Oh, no, something else that will surely die." I put it in the extra bedroom and whenever I thought about it, which wasn't often, I'd toss some water on it. Then, by some miracle, a couple months later the flowers started to bloom. It was *so* meaningful. I felt like Micah's life was acknowledged by that plant.

—Amy

## POINTS TO REMEMBER

- Memories and mementos help you cope. They affirm your baby and let you experience a gradual goodbye; they help you remember this time and feel close to your baby as you grieve.
- Rituals and memorials honor your baby's importance in your life.
- If you have regrets, you need to identify them and express your feelings—perhaps anger, disappointment and sorrow. Remember, you could not have known at the time that certain things would be a comfort to you later.
- It's never too late to memorialize your baby in meaningful, comforting ways.

## 6

# Painful Feelings

Grief encompasses many painful feelings and some are especially difficult to express, cope with and work through. Feelings of failure, anger, guilt and vulnerability to tragedy are common among parents whose baby has died. If you are prone to these feelings in other areas of your life, they may arise more intensely when your baby dies.

Your own tendencies and personality can intensify these feelings, as well as factors associated with fertility, pregnancy, delivery, cause of death and supportive relationships. If it took a long time to get pregnant or if this baby was your only child, you may feel an added sense of failure and vulnerability. If you have been told that future pregnancy is unlikely or a recurrence of genetic defects is probable, you may feel especially angry and wonder, "Why me?" If, on the other hand, the pregnancy was unplanned or if you had a particularly difficult day before tragedy struck, you may feel intensely guilty that your negative feelings somehow caused the baby to die. The particular circumstances surrounding your baby's demise may point to someone or something to blame—or perhaps you blame yourself. This search for answers sharpens the usual feelings of anger or guilt. Lack of a stable intimate relationship or supportive friends and family tends to deepen feelings of anger and failure.

Three of these feelings—anger, guilt and failure—arise from the belief that you are in charge of your destiny. Until a tragedy strikes, you may have thought you had control over what happens to you. You make plans; you follow them. You have goals; you attain them. You place a lot of faith in doctors and other caregivers who have always come through in the past. You may have put your faith in God, fate or universal justice. Many people do this with their health, their finances, their careers, their relationships, their children.

This sense of control is the source of many of your painful feelings. You may be angry that your baby died in spite of happier plans; you may feel guilty you could not prevent it; you may feel there must be something wrong with you that such a terrible thing could happen. You may agonize over the questions "Why me? Why my baby?" You want answers to ensure more control in the future.

Another approach is to realize that you don't always have the power to prevent bad things from happening to you and that misfortune can strike even when you least expect it. This vulnerability to tragedy can be a terrifying feeling to face.

To avoid the fear and helplessness that come with vulnerability, you may want to hold on to anger, guilt or failure for a while. These emotions protect that comfortable illusion of being in total control. Later, as you begin adjusting to your baby's death, you will come to the painful realization that you don't have control over everything that happens in your life.

You may also hold on to anger or guilt as a way to avoid sadness and despair. If grieving is like a roller-coaster, profound sadness and despair are at the bottom of the deepest dips. These emotions are so painful that you may try to build bridges so you don't have to plummet so far down. Feelings like anger and guilt can serve as bridges.

You may wonder, "Why shouldn't I use these bridges to avoid feeling the depths of despair?" Unfortunately, holding on to these feelings forever can be incapacitating. Guilt and failure can eat away at your feelings of self-worth. Anger can interfere with your enjoyment of life. You are entitled to say, "How can I ever feel good about myself and enjoy life—MY BABY IS DEAD!" But as time goes on, you may become weary of being angry or guilty and want to move on. This can be a sign that you are ready to tackle your sadness and despair over your baby's death.

Sadness and despair can be excruciatingly painful. These feelings can make you feel broken, discouraged and overwhelmed. You may be afraid that if you start crying, you may never stop. But, in fact, you may notice that if you really take the time and energy to cry, to think about your baby and your loss, to really feel the pain, then you can also feel relief from holding these powerful emotions inside.

One way that you might try to get in touch with your sadness and despair is to drop the defenses of failure, guilt and anger. First, try to replace the failure or guilt with anger, and then replace the anger with sadness. For example, if you feel failure or guilt about not being with your baby when he or she died, you might try saying, "I feel angry that I wasn't with my baby when he (or she) died." After you say that a while, you might be able to let yourself feel angry. Then, after you are comfortable feeling angry, replace "angry" with "sad" or "hurt": "I feel sad (or hurt) that I wasn't with my baby when he (or she) died." Then let yourself express those painful feelings of sadness.

Parents have found other ways to get in touch with the deep feelings of grief. For several months after her daughter died, Stephanie made sure that every morning before doing anything else, she would look at Jamie's pictures, talk to her, cry and write about her feelings in a journal. She discovered that by doing this she felt better and was able to get through the day more easily. Likewise, Kitty knew that when she was feeling stress, she needed to take the time to go through her "memory box" where she kept pictures and mementos of her baby. Tearfully she would examine the keepsakes. Afterward she would feel better, relieved of the tension. You may discover your own rituals to help you release your deepest feelings of grief.

> There were times when I made it hurt. I'd look at the pictures and I'd want to hurt and I couldn't figure out why, but I guess I knew I needed to grieve. I'd get out the pictures and I'd read stories and I'd go to her grave and I'd cry and I'd hurt. I'd feel the pain like it had just happened. And now I can't feel that pain anymore. I can look at the pictures, I can do everything I would have done a year ago, and it doesn't hurt like it did. It's just, I've dealt with it. If I hadn't done that, the pain would still be in there and I wouldn't even be able to talk about it. And then it would be harder to deal with. I believe that as the years go on, if you don't let it out, it's going to be harder.
>
> —Cindy

> I made myself do what I had to do to get through it. I think the reason I feel as good as I do now is because I made myself grieve for my son, by forcing myself to confront how I was feeling. As your grieving goes on, when you first cry, you cry all the time. After a while you

can stop your tears and put them away, but I *always* took
them back out again and I made myself look at my
picture of Jamie and I made myself read all the literature
and I *made* myself grieve for him. Grieving is not fun. It's
very easy not to, it's very easy to go on, go to the movies
or change the subject. It's something that you have to
force yourself to do, and I think because I did, that is the
reason I feel so much better now.

—Sarah

While some mothers immerse themselves in grief, others bury
themselves in work or extra activities. But the outcomes can be
different: Mothers who give themselves time and permission to grieve
are more likely to feel they are on the road to recovery. Those who
hold back may eventually recognize that their lives are still com-
promised by the grief they have tried to avoid.

Holly, Lena and Anya provide testimony to the fact that grief is
hard work and takes time, but the more it is expressed, the easier it
may be in the long run.

I think I've been in a fog for two entire years. I have
functioned beautifully to the outside world and pulled an
incredible work load and accomplished an incredible
amount of things, but personally I've just been in a fog.
It's amazing to me that I've pulled it off, but I think by
avoiding grief, I've caused myself more agony.

—Holly

I immediately immersed myself in volunteer work as an
escape mechanism. I kept myself so busy that I didn't
have time to think. At the time I think that's what was
needed. I didn't want to wallow in self-pity. I did bury a
lot of my feelings and I'm sure there are some feelings I
haven't even come to grips with. I still feel a little pit in
my stomach when I think about it, so I know there still
must be something there. I probably should go back to
counseling, but I don't have time.

—Lena

I've learned it's OK to let yourself hurt. You may feel that you're falling apart and going crazy, but it's OK. You'll come back together again.

—Anya

# FAILURE

Feelings of failure arise when you believe there was something you could have done better or more competently. If you have trouble conceiving or if there were problems with your uterus, cervix, hormone levels or placenta, you may feel like your body failed you. If the baby was born with genetic anomalies, you and your partner may feel a great sense of failure that your genes are somehow defective. You may question your ability to bear a healthy child or worry that you don't deserve to be parents. You may wonder if you are a failure as a woman or a man.

> I felt really betrayed by my body. I felt like there was something wrong with me physically that I could not complete a pregnancy, and that got to be a goal almost as much as having a baby—to complete a pregnancy successfully. I just really hated my body for a while. I felt like it just wasn't working right.
>
> —Jessie

> I don't like the term *incompetent cervix*. It sounds like I got an F in the class. Incompetent. I've never been incompetent at anything in my life!
>
> —Lena

Some mothers feel an intensified sense of failure because they have experienced prolonged infertility, complicated pregnancies, the death of more than one baby, or the death of one or both twins. Or perhaps they are already raising a child with birth defects.

> I had a lot of problems with each pregnancy and for a long time I thought that I was a sinful person or just one who didn't deserve to have these kids.
>
> —Meryl

Sometimes I've really felt a lot of failure because both my other kids have problems. ... So you know, you just feel like you haven't done anything right. I've felt like I couldn't make a baby right!

—Rayleen

About having babies, I feel like I'm not a pro, let me tell you! The thought of having another baby, trying again, scares the hell out of me. Because of not just Nicole, but the miscarriages and premature births. So I guess I do feel like I'm not the best baby producer.

—Cindy

Horrible feelings of failure—that I couldn't carry a pregnancy to term, that I couldn't keep two babies alive, that my body had bailed out on me. I had tried to do all the things you're supposed to do and it hadn't worked. My next pregnancy went fine, but it wasn't twins. It was a one-baby kind of thing.

—Anya

There are a number of ways mothers have found to cope with and work through these uncomfortable feelings of failure.

- Write in a journal. Just putting feelings down on paper can help you feel better, by freeing you of the burden of holding them inside and perhaps giving you the insights you need to feel better about yourself.
- Renew hobbies and other interests. Go back to work. By engaging in activities in which you feel competent, you can regain feelings of self-worth.
- Talk to someone. It helps to talk to someone who is supportive—your partner, a good friend, a clergyperson or a counselor who can accept your feelings and reassure you that you are still a good mother and a good person.
- Accept yourself and your body. Many bereaved mothers learn to accept that they are imperfect. It is healthier to realize you are imperfect than to always strive to be perfect. Perfection is never achieved, whereas imper-

fection allows you to feel good and worthy for just who you are.

For many mothers, having another baby helps to boost feelings of competence and success. They acquire some faith in themselves again and abandon the idea that there is something wrong with their body, personality or soul. Dara talks about how relieved and reassured she felt: "That we could have a healthy baby was a big thing. With Laurie, the relief was the greatest, being able to have a normal female."

Remember, bad things happen to good people without stripping them of their goodness. Regardless of what has happened to you, you are still a worthwhile person and a good mother who deserves the best life has to offer.

# ANGER

Anger is a powerful feeling that may consume you at times. It is normal to feel angry at medical technology or the doctors and nurses. Could they have prevented your baby's death? It is normal to feel angry at the world, fate, God or Mother Nature. It is normal to feel angry at pregnant women in general, especially those who seem to produce healthy babies effortlessly despite abominable habits during pregnancy. Sophie remarks, "I'd see or hear about moms that smoke and drink too much when they're pregnant and they have these perfectly healthy babies. I had a perfectly healthy pregnancy and I ate all my proteins and my vegetables and vitamins, and Stephanie wasn't here. It seemed so unfair."

You may also resent mothers with healthy babies, especially if you think they are not being as kind and nurturing as you imagine yourself to be. You may wonder, "Why do other mothers get to keep their babies when I am equally or more deserving than they are?" You may even feel anger at your baby. As Erin admits, "Sometimes I'm a little resentful toward my baby for doing this to me. It wasn't very fair of her." It is unfair to carry a baby—whether for three months or nine or into infancy—only to be cheated, denied from keeping him or her.

Thanksgiving came and I was screaming mad, saying, "What do I have to be thankful for!" because I had lost

David, then had a miscarriage and then I wasn't pregnant
and was having trouble getting pregnant and I felt there
was nothing to be thankful for. I had lost my baby and
that was the cruelest thing ever. I felt so cheated that we
had wanted that baby so badly and we were going to be
such wonderful parents and then to have him taken away.
… I shouldn't have carried a baby full term and then not
be able to keep him. The point is, he should be with us
right now, we should all be together and he's still not
with us, so I think that part is always going to hurt
because he'll never be with us.

—Bess

I could not hold a baby. I didn't want to be around babies
and anyone that had a baby. I wanted to shoot them. It
was a terrible feeling. That's why I think having Robin
has helped a lot because now I've got another baby, and
now other people can have babies too and it's OK, but
back then it wasn't.

—Martina

Being around pregnant women or babies can be intolerable. It
arouses the resentment and envy you have, drawing attention to the
fact that another person has a baby and you don't. You may try to
avoid them, but they appear almost everywhere you go.

You may also feel angry at the circumstances that surrounded
your baby's death: the medical care you received, the lack of
information, or the fact that you were not encouraged to hold your
baby at all or weren't offered more time with your baby or did not
receive a photograph or other mementos. Someone may suggest that
you bring a lawsuit against the hospital or the doctors, but most
parents agree with Desi: " … that's not going to bring the baby back."

I was very angry, boy was I mad. I bet I was *nothing* but
mad for like a week. I was just furious. I was furious at
everything. I was furious at the weather. I was so mad about
this particular thing, beta strep. Two years before my son
was born they decided to stop testing for it routinely
because it was statistically insignificant, the number of

babies who got that. That made me so mad I just kept getting madder and madder, and I was just so sad. It was just awful. It was the worst thing I've ever gone through.

—Sarah

It's bad enough when your baby dies, but the care we got afterwards was just horrible. ... They weren't that smart at this particular hospital. My Lamaze teacher dropped off the book *When Hello Means Goodbye* that made me realize that I should do all these things, like having a picture ... I wanted these things, and the next morning I asked for mementos ... they said it was too late.

—Holly

I still feel angry that we didn't go up to visit the baby in the hospital. I wish now we had. ... Nobody encouraged us to. We had planned to go up on the weekend and Elisa died on Friday, and it never occurred to us really to go up after she died. ... Now I think my anger is not that it happened, but now it's the things I wish I'd known to do then that I know I would do now.

—Dara

One of the best ways to cope with anger is to find constructive ways to express it. Many people hold in their anger, for fear that its expression will be too destructive. Indeed, expressing anger in destructive ways only makes things worse because you have to deal with the consequences—feeling pain, needing to apologize, cleaning up, buying costly replacements. Unfortunately, holding in anger is not a solution—it can result in prolonged depression, ill health, hurtful outbursts, substance abuse or other compulsive behaviors. Remember, you are entitled to nasty, angry feelings and fantasies. Don't try to control your emotions and thoughts, control your *behavior*. Express your feelings in ways that will not hurt you, other people or valued property. There are a number of nondestructive ways parents have found to express and work through their anger.

- Engage in vigorous exercise. Even a brisk walk can help reduce tension.

- Write an angry letter (you don't have to mail it) to anyone: to your doctor, to God, to fate, to your baby.
- Write in a journal about your angry feelings and thoughts or your fantasies about destructive, vengeful acts.
- Draw a picture that depicts your anger or the revenge you seek.
- Work with clay or Play-Doh; kneading, punching and sculpting can offer release.
- Throw a ball up against a wall.
- Punch pillows.
- Drape a rug over a clothesline and beat it with a broom handle.
- Beat a towel against a hard surface.
- Yank the weeds out of your garden.
- Throw things, such as plastic containers and other nonbreakables.
- Scream and yell when you are alone.
- Talk to your partner or a friend who can support and validate your anger.
- Talk to other bereaved parents who share your anger.

These methods have helped many parents cope with angry feelings. You may find your own effective, nondestructive ways to express anger. By acknowledging and expressing it, you can perhaps move closer toward resolution.

> I practiced expressing anger this week. I threw the adding machine tape, I threw plastic bottles down the stairs, I yelled at a solicitor for baby products on the phone. When I felt angry, I took it out right then on whatever was at hand.
>
> —Janet

## GUILT

Along with failure and anger, guilt arises from the belief that you are in total control of your life. When you are pregnant, you take good care of yourself in the belief that if you are healthy, follow your doctor's advice, avoid consuming dangerous substances and monitor your baby's every move, you will deliver a healthy baby. When you do have a healthy baby, you vow to comfort and protect this child for as long as you live.

When fate takes an unexpected, tragic direction, you may wonder if there was something you did or did not do that may have contributed to your baby's death. It is natural to feel primarily responsible for your baby's well-being. Because that baby was inside your body or under your protective care, you may have fantasies about what you might have done to prevent this loss. When you believe you should have total control, it is easy to feel angry at yourself when everything seems to go wrong.

> My initial reaction was, of course, "What did I do? I know I must be responsible for this and what could it have been?" So I felt guilty, but I didn't know quite how to focus that guilt because I didn't know what I had done. I had a wonderful pediatrician who actually called me a month and a half later to make sure that I wasn't feeling guilty. And the neonatologist and obstetrician kept laying facts in front of me and saying, "There is *no way* that you were responsible for this. You couldn't be responsible." They helped me through that.
>
> —Sarah

> I felt as though either I had done something to deserve this baby dying or I had done something physically to cause her death or that there was something wrong with me that they hadn't noticed. ... I felt the guilt any parent feels when something happens to their child. You're responsible for that child and you're supposed to protect them and take care of them, and I felt like I had fallen down on the job.
>
> —Jessie

Even when your doctor reassures you that there was nothing you could have done differently or even if you *know* that your baby's death is not your fault, you may still have nagging feelings that there was something you should have done differently or that you let your baby down in some way. Especially if you tend to get angry at yourself over things that happen, you are likely to feel some guilt about your baby. Some mothers feel guilty for ever being aggravated with the baby or that they somehow failed to be a good mother. Some mothers think they are getting paid back for "bad" things they've done in the past. Others feel guilty because of difficult decisions, such as terminating the pregnancy or disconnecting life-support systems. Sarah sums up her guilt: "I wasn't there to hold him when he died— I failed him. I had all these hormones that were trying to be mothering and here was my big opportunity and I blew it. And everybody said, 'Well, he didn't know if you were there or not.' But who knows? I felt like I really failed him."

Because guilt is anger toward yourself, it can be self-destructive. It doesn't allow you to feel good about yourself and can be a source of chronic depression. It may even make you wonder if you deserved this tragedy. But, of course, nobody deserves the tragedy of having a baby die. Unfortunately, bad things can happen to anyone, without warning. We cannot always avoid tragedy or know ahead of time the right course of action.

Working through feelings of guilt can be difficult. You need to

- let yourself off the hook,
- accept that you did the best you could,
- remember that you made the best decisions you could based on information available,
- realize you cannot always prevent bad things from happening, and
- talk to others who can reassure you that you are not to blame.

You want to control things. You feel like you should be able to control things. Did I do something wrong? People would tell me if you lift your arms above your head, that it's supposed to choke your baby or something. And that was a bunch of ... that was so stupid. But all those things went through my mind. Did I ever lift my arms up? Did I ever bend over wrong? You know, *what did I do?* And I didn't do anything. It took a long time and I just realized, she would have died regardless of what I did. And me rolling around on the floor is not going to tie her cord in

a knot, that was Nicole's doing. I couldn't have reached
my hands in there and untied it or know—how could I
know unless I had an ultrasound machine, and even then
you can't see the cord. There's no way that anybody
could've known.

—Cindy

I think that you feel out of control with almost any death,
when you realize that we don't have control. I mean, that
we do and we don't. I go back and forth on that. ... Right
after Heidi died I'd been confronted about my guilt over
her death, and I go back and forth between wanting to
take responsibility and saying, "Hey, come on, I did not
cause this, this cannot be my responsibility."

—Holly

I wallowed in guilt for a long time. I elicited feedback
from other people to the contrary—my therapist, my
husband—and I commiserated with other mothers from
the support group who understood that feeling. I still feel
guilty every once in a while. I think that I've mostly let go
of it because even if there was anything I could have done,
I think that right now I feel like there was, but that's past
history and right now it's not going to do me any good—
or my baby any good—to stay stuck in that place.

—Jessie

Even if you have a strong feeling that you did something wrong,
you can still get to a point where you accept the fact that you made
a mistake, an error in judgment, and forgive yourself for being
imperfect.

They were going to disconnect the life support and asked
if we wanted to be there, and I said, "No." What a
LOUSY decision that was, but I did the best I could. ...
But for two years I beat myself up for that a million times
over. For probably a good year and a half, I didn't even
really deal with my guilt. It was so painful to me that it
wasn't until way towards the end of my real grieving time

that I was even strong enough to cope with that. It was
just admitting to myself that I had done this stupid thing.
It was awful. ... I probably worked on it for six weeks in
therapy, where I was finally able to let myself off the
hook for it. Now I'm able to objectively say I did the best
I could in that situation. I would never do it again and a
part of me still wishes I hadn't done that.

—Sarah

I felt guilty at first. It took me a long time to work
through that. I was very active and at times I've felt like,
"Gee, if I had REALLY rested and if I had really stayed in
bed, this probably wouldn't have happened." To this day
I could probably say to you that I still feel maybe if I had
followed the rules a little bit more, I probably wouldn't
have lost the baby. But, you know, I feel that that was me
at the time, like it was a different person back then and
she could have probably done a lot of things to make the
pregnancy better but she didn't, and I forgive her.

—Elaine

Some mothers work through their guilt by eventually turning
their anger away from themselves and toward someone else, making
their anger less destructive to their self-esteem. Many mothers turn
their anger toward their obstetrician or pediatrician, fate or God.

I felt guilty. But the only reason I blamed myself was
because I was the only person who had contact with the
baby, so I must have been the reason why he died. ... I
couldn't blame God because I needed Him too much to
lean on, so then finally after going to the support group I
got to where I blamed the doctor, and that's where I've
stayed.

—Desi

It was my first pregnancy and I didn't know, I thought my
labor was starting. I called the hospital and said, "I'm
getting really weird pains. I think maybe I should be
checked. I don't know what's going on." The doctor said,

"Don't worry about it." And I still am mad about that
because I think, "If I would've gone in, they would have
seen the stress and they would have gotten her out."

—Cindy

Remember, whatever reasoning you come up with, YOU DID
THE BEST YOU COULD AT THE TIME. Like most mothers, you
are incapable of knowingly endangering your baby. Working through
feelings of guilt involves realizing that you cannot always prevent
tragedy from happening and that you cannot always avoid making
mistakes.

# VULNERABILITY

As you come to terms with your feelings of failure, anger and guilt, you
will realize that life is unfair and that you are vulnerable to tragedy. The
question "Why me, why my baby?" is one you may never answer. This
can be frustrating, because if you had known why it happened, then
maybe you could have prevented it. It makes you feel helpless to be told
that nothing in particular should have been done differently. As Hannah
reports, "It felt like a bolt out of the sky."

Many parents simply come to accept the fact that horrible things
sometimes happen. Rose notes, "If you think you're protected, it's a
real comforting feeling, but you're just naive. Some people go
through their whole lives without anything bad happening to them.
It just means they're lucky, and when something bad does happen, I
guess people try to interpret it a million ways, but I think it just
happens." While this feeling of vulnerability can make you feel
defeated or afraid, you will eventually find a balance between
maintaining control over your life and accepting the limitations.

When I asked, "Why me?" I don't know that I ever got an
answer. At first I blamed the doctor because he didn't
care. Now I just feel like it was fate. You don't know
what to think, but that's kind of where I've left it.

—Erin

This experience was good for me in the sense that it
taught me that you can't think that things go a certain

way just necessarily because you do all the right things.

—Anya

When it first happened, I was terrified of the future. I couldn't stand the thought of bad things happening in my life. Well, now that it's been four years and nothing bad has happened, I have Leslie now, and everything's been positive. That makes it much easier to deal with it. But I'm still afraid.

—Bryn

You really feel like you don't have any control anymore, and there is a real loss of ego there. For a while I just felt like I shouldn't make any plans because something could happen and it could just wipe everything away. Now I feel more confident. I feel like I might as well make a lot of plans and if they don't work out, at least I had the enjoyment of making them.

—Rose

## POINTS TO REMEMBER

- Feelings of anger, guilt and failure arise from the belief that you are always in control of your destiny.
- You can find healthy ways to express and cope with these feelings. If you feel angry, learn to express it in nondestructive ways. If you feel guilty, learn to forgive yourself. Nobody is perfect; nobody can predict the future. If you feel failure, learn to reassure yourself that you are worthwhile.
- For a while, these feelings of anger, guilt or failure can shield you from feelings of deep sadness or vulnerability, but eventually, holding on to them will become incapacitating.
- Getting in touch with your deep sadness and despair is difficult, but it frees you from the destructive clutches of anger, guilt and failure.
- Accept human vulnerability. Tragedies occur, and we don't have control over everything that happens to us.
- Eventually you will find a balance between maintaining control over your life and accepting its limitations.

# 7

# Resolution of Grief

A resolution of grief occurs when you are able to accept the fact that your baby is gone and integrate this loss appropriately into your life. Resolution does *not* signal an end to grief. You will always feel longing and sadness. Eventually, though, these feelings may mellow to the point that you can feel peaceful when you remember your baby.

As resolution brings some relief from mourning, it enables you to move on with your life in healthy, functional ways. You can find happiness, reinvest your energy in satisfying relationships and pursuits, and feel a renewed sense of hope for the future.

At first, it may seem impossible to accept and integrate your baby's death into your life. In the midst of overwhelming despair, it is difficult to imagine ever being able to think about your baby and the circumstances surrounding the death without suffering. But, as the intensity of the experience fades, acceptance can feel comfortable. Bereaved parents often consider this the hallmark of resolution.

> Just gradually over time it felt for the most part that I could accept it, I could live with it, it was not nearly as painful. It's something I feel sad about and I have regrets that it happened, but it's not anything I feel angry or guilty about anymore. It hurts, but it's OK—an important point to get to and it's not a point I could have understood, I think, before she died, that something can hurt horribly but it's all right.
>
> —Anya

Some parents mistakenly equate a lack of emotional pain with the completion of grief work. Although they say they *feel* resolved, they are hiding from their own feelings, as if there is nothing to be sad about or as though it happened to someone else. This avoidance can create other problems, including substance abuse or failure to maintain nurturing relationships. (See chapter 2, "Numbness and Shock.")

At the opposite extreme, there are parents who hold on to their grief as a way of giving their life meaning, or as a way to hold on to the baby. Some parents worry that if they stop feeling angry about their baby's death, then somehow they're admitting defeat. Others believe that if they are not despondent, they are being disloyal or desecrating their baby's life. By holding on to these grieving patterns, some parents feel reassured that they will never forget their baby.

It is important to recognize that you can remember, love and miss your baby without grieving continuously. You can go ahead in life without forgetting your past.

> Sometimes I feel happy or proud, and other times just sad. It's all mixed. I can have good thoughts about her, kind of a resolved thing. Even when I feel grief it's not a desperate feeling, it's a comfortable feeling. I know she's dead and I can't get her back. I don't have those Oh–I–can't–stand–it–get–her–back–here! feelings as if I could pull her out of the air if I had enough faith, if I gritted my teeth hard enough or whatever. I can't describe exactly how I feel because it's always up and down, but resolved means I can look at her picture and not burst into tears. ... She's just one of my daughters. The subject is pretty much closed. There's nothing to say. It's all over. I can't bring her back. But it's definitely not like I've put her in a closet and closed the door.
>
> —Rose

> It's a relief. I feel peaceful. I know he's with God and my tormenting is over, but I still love him. He's not forgotten. That's another thing I was afraid of. I thought, "I've got to keep this up, keep grieving so that I don't forget him. I don't want anybody to forget him." But you don't have to be miserable to remember.
>
> —Desi

# THE JOURNEY TO RESOLUTION

## *HOW LONG WILL IT TAKE?*

Although there is no definite time frame, resolution can take several years. Within the first year or two, many mothers report that the initial hard edges of pain gradually soften. Over time they notice that they don't cry as easily or they are able to look at infants or pregnant women without acute envy. As sad as it is, this experience becomes something to live with on a private, interior level. Martina found that it became less difficult to think or talk about her baby. She remarks, "When I think about him it's not something that is so bold like it was before, that when you start thinking about him you just have to stop everything because you're in a daze for a week." Sarah noticed that instead of focusing on her baby's death, it became a part of her history, a part that will always exist but one that no longer occupies center stage. Peg agrees: "It fades a little bit to the background. I still think about the twins quite a bit and I'm sad and I wish that it hadn't happened, but it just doesn't hurt as much as time goes on."

After your emotional pain fades and your concentration shifts, feelings of acceptance and integration follow. When your grief ceases to tear at you and the longing subsides, you will find that you can have happy thoughts about your baby's short life. Jessie notes, "Now it feels like an unfortunate event that changed me forever. I'll always remember her and be sad that she's not living with us, but happy that we had her for a while." Meryl remarks, "The yearning, the little bit of grief will always be there, but I don't feel it that much anymore. I feel at peace, it's just accepted, it's OK."

Unfortunately, the roller-coaster ride to resolution is a bumpy one, and there are no shortcuts. The softening of grief and the acceptance of your tragedy don't always build in a smooth, steady progression. There are ups and downs and heartache along the way, whether it takes several months or several years. Anya remembers the first day she didn't cry for Rachel—seven months after her death. She admits, "I never would have thought it would take that long." Cindy remembers the first year as the worst: " ... the depression, the ups and downs, probably lasted three years. ... Then, as the years go on, it gets easier. People would tell me it gets better with time, but that first year I was sure I would feel that way until I died."

Liza also remembers feeling much better after the first year, but still distrusting the ups because, "as soon as I'd feel really good one day, then almost for sure I'd be right back as bad as ever the next day. It took another year before I felt like there was any plateau." Even so, in the third year, she notes, "I could have a good month and then something would happen, and I'd feel like I was right back again." Bryn remembers it took her a full three years before she could be happy for pregnant friends or see newborn babies. Sarah, five years later, can finally enjoy watching "tearjerker" movies again. She says, "The crying stops when the sad part is over. I can cry again and not be afraid of crying ... just tears for fun." Maya, also five years down the road, describes her experience this way: "Grief is like working on this giant jigsaw puzzle. You work very hard to put it together, and every now and then it feels like it's thrown up in the air and it comes down in pieces. Again, you put it back together, but it's not as bad as starting over, and you may even put it back together a little better."

## IS IT OK TO FEEL UNRESOLVED?

If you are unable to find a comfortable place for your baby and the grief you feel, you may simply need more time to work through all the painful emotions. Your grief may be too fresh for you to feel at peace. You may believe you will never be able to accept your baby's death because, as Bess says, " 'Accepted' means you go along with it." Bryn agrees: "I did not want to accept that this bad thing had happened and that I was going to have to live with this terrible thing for the rest of my life."

It may be hard to find anything positive in this experience. You may believe that your baby's death will never make sense. Hannah notes, "I can't say what it means or that it was meant to be—that just doesn't fit for me. I just think it's always going to be sad."

In spite of what people may tell you, there is no hard evidence to support the idea that feeling unresolved is bad or pathological or unhealthy in itself. As you work through the denial, yearning, anger, guilt, sadness, hurt and despair, naturally you feel unresolved. Yet this is a relatively healthy state of affairs, because you are facing grief instead of hiding from it; you are heading toward resolution instead of circumventing it. It may take several years to reach resolution, but in the meantime, life goes on and you learn to live with anger, sadness and the natural protest against this tragedy.

So although your grief may be unresolved and you may even wish you could feel better, if you can face your grief most of the time, if you are able to express a wide range of feelings and if you feel you are making progress as time goes on, then you may be on your way toward resolution.

On the other hand, if you feel as though you are fighting grief, hiding from it or hanging on to it, you may not be making progress toward resolution. Laura and Holly feel this keenly:

I feel like there's a fire-breathing dragon in a box and I'm tossing drops of water on it and trying to force the lid shut. I'm fighting grief, not at peace.

—Laura

It is frustrating to me to think that although I know the pain or the caring never goes away, in a sense I think it should be easier for me now, or I wonder, "Am I hanging on to this and being more negative or sad than is healthy or than I should be?"

—Holly

## HOW DO I RESOLVE MY GRIEF?

To resolve your grief, you must go through the grieving process, that is, work through your denial, anger, guilt, hurt, despair and other painful feelings. By grieving, you can come to terms with your loss and eventually learn to accept that your baby is gone and adjust to a new life without your baby.

It is natural to want to avoid painful feelings, but there is no way around grief. In order to heal, you must go through it, experiencing and expressing all your difficult feelings. In this way, reaching resolution depends on the quality of your grief work. There are a number of ways to ensure that you work through the grieving process.

- Have realistic expectations about yourself and grieving. If you are informed about what to expect and what is normal for a grieving person, you are more apt to have the patience and tolerance for your reactions and emotions. Recognize that your grief is exactly that—*yours*. Do not let others decide how you should feel. Don't measure your grief against anyone else's. You need to find your own path and do what is best for *you*.

- Give yourself permission to experience all of your emotions and thoughts. Some of these may seem unacceptable to you, but if you have them, *you are entitled to them*. By burying or avoiding them, you only give them more power to compromise your life and your happiness. By expressing them constructively, you empower yourself to get through grief and eventually make life meaningful again. Rationalizing or intellectualizing them won't suffice. You must express your emotions from your heart and your gut, not just your mind.

- Identify all your different emotions. Separating them makes them more manageable and easier to cope with, instead of burdening you with a huge, confusing mixture of pain. By focusing on individual emotions, you may also figure out their source and get to the bottom of what you are feeling. Label your emotions specifically— anger, guilt, anxiety, despair. Once you do this you can start finding relief from them. You may also need to uncover the anger, hurt and other feelings from previous losses—the unfinished grief from your past. By lessening this emotional confusion, you can express and work through your feelings instead of getting stuck or going around in circles.

- Dwell on your memories and your hopes and dreams of what might have been. By reviewing your experiences and your fantasies, you can identify what you have lost and then gradually let go of your emotional investment. You may need to remember and talk about these memories and expectations over and over as you adjust to the fact that your baby is gone and your life has changed. At first, idealizing your baby is normal. Eventually it will be important for you to remember the good times and the bad and to recognize that no baby is the perfect child. Having a realistic image of your baby can ease the letting go. This eventual letting go is what enables you to focus your emotional energy toward a new future.

- Identify the things you regret not doing with your baby and find appropriate ways to have closure. For instance, if you did not have a chance to hold your baby or show your love in certain ways, you will need to express your sorrow or find ways to express this love. You may want to talk about how you feel with supportive friends or other bereaved parents, write a letter to your baby, or go to the grave or the place where you scattered or keep the ashes and talk to your baby. If you had looked forward to experiencing special occasions or the holiday season with your baby, you can engage in rituals that let you feel close to your baby: Lighting a candle, displaying an ornament, reading a special poem or making donations in your baby's name are all ways to give meaning to these times when you especially miss your baby.

- Take care of yourself as you grieve. Give yourself opportunities to be alone and cry. Be patient with yourself. Allow for the time and energy it takes and for your uneven progress. Find ways to reduce stress, including good nutrition, exercise, relaxation and giving yourself breaks from grief—allowing yourself to enjoy other aspects of your life. For at least the first year, avoid making significant changes in your life. Major changes may only increase your stress and multiply the adjustments you must make.

- Get the social support you need. Grieving in isolation is more painful and makes reaching resolution more difficult. Let others help and nurture you. You deserve their comfort and kindness. At the same time, be assertive and tell people what you need. Don't expect them to read your mind. Find people who can listen and accept your feelings and thoughts. (See chapter 9, "Support Networks.")

- Have realistic ideas about what resolution means. Remember that you aren't giving up or forgetting your baby. Resolution doesn't mean you will never feel grief again or that you are glad this happened, nor does it mean you will return to the way things were before. Continued suffering and misery are not proof of your devotion to your baby. Healthy grief and resolution mean adjusting to a new future while remembering and finding appropriate ways to feel connected to your baby.

## HOW DO I KNOW IF I AM REACHING RESOLUTION?

Bereavement experts such as John Bowlby, Edgar Jackson, Colin Murray Parkes, Therese Rando and Simon Rubin recommend completing the following processes over the months and years after your baby dies, so you can successfully resolve your grief.

- Acknowledge your loss. Have you acknowledged that your baby is dead and will never return to life? Or do you sustain a flicker of hope that there has been a terrible mistake and your baby can be recovered?
- Understand how your baby died. Do you have an explanation for how your baby died that you can accept, whether it can be proven or not? Or do you still wonder what caused your baby's death?
- Accept all your feelings. Have you found comfortable ways to express your various emotions? Or do you avoid feelings that seem inappropriate or irrational?
- Experience the hurt and sadness. Have you felt your deepest feelings of despair? Or are you still hiding behind anger, guilt, failure or numbness?
- Change your expectations for the future. Have you modified the hopes and dreams that involved this child? Or do you still hold on to what might have been or depend on your baby to give your life meaning?
- Readjust to life without your baby. Have you found other ways to be happy, perhaps other people or activities to enjoy? Or do you still feel empty and unable to find fulfillment or satisfaction in your baby's absence?
- Change your emotional investment in your baby. Are you able to remember or talk about your baby without feeling overwhelmed? Or do thoughts of your baby bring up acute feelings of grief?
- Form a new relationship with your baby. Are you able to think of your baby in terms of what might have been without acting on those fantasies? Or do you act as if your baby is still with you?
- Think of your baby realistically. Can you think about your baby in terms of negative and positive qualities? Or

do you idealize your baby, only remembering or super-imposing positive qualities?

- Maintain an appropriate connection to your baby. Are you able to recognize your baby's impact on your life and remember and do those things that enhance your life? Or do you continue to retain connections that compromise your happiness or spontaneity? (Example: You still enjoy going on a daily walk, but you don't always stop at the playground and push the swing your baby liked.)

- Reinvest your emotional energy. Can you establish and maintain fulfilling relationships with other people or pursue rewarding activities? Or do you refrain from getting involved in close relationships or satisfying activities?

In the early months after your baby dies, you cannot expect yourself to have worked through any of these processes. You can think of these as goals to strive toward or you can check this list every few months to get an idea of your progress. If you notice that you have made headway through some but not all of these processes, this list may help you focus your energy on those that are keeping you unresolved or unadjusted to your baby's absence.

*WHAT DOES RESOLUTION FEEL LIKE AT FIRST?*
For many mothers, resolution appears on the horizon when thinking about the baby is less painful. Eventually, happy feelings are more prevalent than sad ones. Feelings of peace and acceptance creep up, and perhaps silver linings can be appreciated. Sophie feels a glimmer of resolution: "I don't think I'll ever completely accept it, but it has mellowed. Sometimes I feel sad and other times I can feel peaceful about it all and look at the positive effect she had on me." Cindy and Liza recall when they started feeling resolved:

> I think I got to a point where I thought, "My baby died, that's the way it is, and I can't change it and I better quit wishing it would change. It can't; it won't. So I have to deal with it, go on."
>
> —Cindy

I began to realize that love isn't limited. The more you
give away, the more you have. Instead of being angry at
everybody else because they didn't die when he died—
that's the way I felt, that the whole world should've
stopped—I began to see that other people have pain
whether I think it was as great as mine or not. There were
a lot of selfish feelings, like "Nobody has ever gone
through something like this," but I began to realize that
it's a universal thing and to really feel more love for
people because of that. Once you have a little resolution
you start to see what the rest of the world is going
through.

—Liza

# MAKING SENSE OF TRAGEDY

### *RECOGNIZING THE POSITIVE*

After your baby dies, trying to find something positive is one way to
make sense of your tragedy. At first, you may be too distraught or too
angry to even consider anything positive. But when you start to feel
better, you can try to assess the salvage from the wreckage. Unfortunately, other people may try to help you make sense of it. They may
try to point out something positive about your baby's death by saying
things like, "At least the baby died before you were too far along ... "
or "It's a blessing the baby died because ... " or "Be thankful that at
least you know you can get pregnant." This method of comfort may
seem cruel to you, but people are simply anxious to help you feel
better and hasten you along with well-meaning speeches.

Eventually, when you are ready, you may recognize something
positive from the experiences surrounding your loss. Perhaps you will
find you have a strengthened marriage, deepened friendships, increased personal awareness, greater confidence or better understanding
of and willingness to help others who experience loss. You may even
have a new baby, who might not have been conceived if the other
baby had lived. These positive things do not make up for your baby's
death, but you may derive some small comfort from them. Your own
philosophies and outlook on life may determine whether you eventually find comfort in recognizing anything positive from the tragedy
of your baby's death.

The time we had with Jamie was so brief, but now I can
look back on that and smile. And I didn't think I'd ever
smile about that. Every time I thought about that, it
would make me cry. But now I'm grateful that I had that
time, that I had him for three days, instead of none.

—Sarah

Something good has to come out of it, because I don't
want her death to be totally in vain. I don't want it to be
totally meaningless. So I try to use every opportunity to
talk about her and help other people who are going
through the same thing. I have a desire for something
good to come out of it. I know I'm a better mother than I
probably would have been.

—Rose

For some parents, the positives may remain elusive. Holly
comments, "I can sort of accept that it was a learning process and that
you grow through pain and all that. But I just don't think anybody
needs that learning process." Bryn agrees: "I led a very lucky life. I
always had the philosophy that, 'Hey, everything works out for the
best.' I cannot have that philosophy anymore, because I will never be
able to say it was best that he died. I can *never* say that."

### WHY ME, WHY MY BABY?

Another way to try to make sense of it all is to figure out "Why me,
why my baby?" Aside from autopsy reports and medical theories
about *how* your baby died, you need answers about *why* this had to
happen at all.

The doctors said that it was just some stray molecule of
bacteria in the air that Rachel breathed, and it gave her
meningitis, like she was at the wrong place at the wrong
time and breathed the wrong breath. What are the
chances? Why did everything come together so wrong?

—Carolyn

Eventually you may find acceptable answers. Upon getting
pregnant so easily after Scott's death, Kelly decided that perhaps

there was a divine plan at work in her life. Jane simply accepts that God gives her the children He wants her to have, enabling her to accept the fact that "this baby was not the one He wanted for me to have." Originally, Jessie wondered what she had done "to deserve such a horrible thing," but now she believes that there was some unknown purpose. She says, "Maybe her soul wasn't ready, maybe that was just as long as she was supposed to be with us. I do believe that it changed things, that because of her, Kent and I really developed our relationship and stayed together. So it helps me to think that maybe that was part of the purpose."

Perhaps you believe there is no plan, no single purpose. Maybe we are victims of random events in an imperfect world. For instance, Bess believes that David's death "was purely an accident of nature," while Martina concludes, "I don't think you ever find out why it happened. You just know it did and you've got to live with it." Sarah has decided to stop asking, "Why me?" because "it doesn't get you anywhere."

Whatever your conclusions, you will probably acquire some understanding of why this happened and come to the realization that you don't control your life as much as you thought you did. While this can be an unsettling thought, most parents learn to live with it.

## ANNIVERSARY REACTIONS

You may find that you have particularly bad days at certain times of the year. These "anniversary reactions" are normal responses to the grief of anniversaries relevant to your baby's life and death. Years after your loss, whether you feel resolved or not, you may experience anniversary reactions one or more times a year—around the baby's due date, birth date, death date or holidays such as Memorial Day, Thanksgiving, Mother's Day or Christmas or Hanukkah. Anniversary dates are special *and* painful.

> On the anniversary date of his birth, we always try and
> do something together as a family. I remember on the day
> that would have been his third birthday, being struck with
> the fact that there will always be somebody missing.
> There will always be one less child in my life.
>
> —Sarah

I wish they didn't have Mother's Day! That's the day I
really acknowledge that I have two kids. I'm the mother
of two kids, not just one.

—Cindy

Right after your baby dies, you may feel especially blue every
week on the day of your baby's birth or death. As time goes on, you
may feel depressed on a certain day of each month. You may feel
sad on your own birthday or wistfully think about how old your
child would have been on the first day of every school year. You
may feel particularly forgetful, disorganized, clumsy or even be prone
to accidental injuries, so use extra caution during these stressful
times.

This baby was born on Christmas Eve, and the first year I
was anxious about it, but I think, really, for the first three
years, Christmas was *very* hard. I think when Thanksgiving hit I just immediately tightened up. I knew I had to
manage these things and I would work even harder to get
my Christmas stuff done, and as Christmas approached it
got worse and worse and worse. I just don't like that time
of year anymore.

—Meryl

In October, I'm real mellow and mopey, and on her
birthday it's like, we know it's that day. We take the time
to remember that she was with us at one point... . It's just
like a signal in your body. And I'll break down and cry
over nothing. October is like a lead balloon.

—Erin

Perhaps you fear anniversaries that loom in the distance, like
Yolanda who says, "I'm afraid that after my due date it will really hit
me that I don't have my baby, because that's when I should have him
in my arms. I'm bracing myself."

Anniversary reactions can be discouraging, especially as time
goes on and you feel as though you're putting your life back together.
You may be surprised by the appearance of these emotions. Anniversary reactions can also be unpredictable. It is important to give

yourself permission to have bad days whenever they appear. You are entitled to your own special pattern of grieving.

## THINKING ABOUT WHAT MIGHT HAVE BEEN

At times you may catch yourself thinking or wondering about what the baby would be like now if he or she had lived. At first these thoughts are painful, but eventually, as you let go of your emotional investment in these fantasies, hopes and dreams, they can take on a feeling of wistfulness or curiosity. You may feel this curiosity when you see children who were born at the same time as your baby who died, or in a pensive moment with a subsequent child as you realize the experiences you have missed with the child who died. Surviving twins are a constant reminder.

> We think mostly about what he'd look like and what he'd be doing now. Every year when school starts and at Christmas time I think about how old he is, and I've thought that I'll be thinking about that when he would have graduated from high school, that he would have gotten married, maybe gone to college.
>
> —Martina

> I'll always grieve the "firsts." What would have been the first step, the first word, the first day of school.
>
> —Cathryn

## KEYS TO SURVIVAL

The simple passage of time may prove to be one of your greatest keys to survival. Other resources to fall back on may include your other children, your partner, your family and friends, books, work, religion, hope and an inner strength that you may have only just discovered through this tragedy. To best utilize these resources, be assertive in telling people what you need and pursue the things that help you cope.

The hope of someday having a healthy baby may help you to look ahead. Peg elaborates: "I'm sure that if I hadn't been able to have one that I'd feel entirely different about the whole thing. Having a baby has helped me to deal with it."

The most significant key to your survival may be a conscious choice to get through your grief without letting it destroy your life. You can decide whether you will triumph over it or surrender to it. Many mothers mention reaching a point where they just decide to stop wishing it didn't happen and start learning to live with it.

> You just realize that's the way life is. There's a lot of things we don't like and a lot of things that aren't fair... . You can't change it, so you just deal with it so you can move on. What else can you do? If you don't, then you lose yourself.
>
> —Cindy

## GETTING HELP

At some point you may decide you would like to talk to a professional counselor. If you feel as though you need help reaching resolution, this is an excellent reason to go. You may decide on counseling if you feel as though sufficient time has passed and you still have intense emotional reactions or your thoughts, behavior or physical symptoms are interfering with your ability to progress through grief. (See "Counseling" in chapter 9.)

> For a long time I thought this was as far as I could get, that's just how it was for me. Now, I feel like I need to get to a different place, need to move on. It doesn't feel like I want it to be, like, a part of my life. It's still too painful. I want to go to a better place, be at peace with it. So I'm back in therapy.
>
> —Laura

## POINTS TO REMEMBER

- Resolved grief is marked by acceptance and integration of the loss into your life: Intense grief has mellowed into bittersweet or peaceful feelings and you acquire a renewed interest in relationships and pleasurable activities. Resolution allows you to live for a new future instead of dwelling on the past or what might have been.
- Resolution also includes sadness, love and remembrance.
- Unresolved grief is accompanied by an inability to accept your loss, repression of or continuing feelings of grief, and the baby's life and death occupying a central part of your life.
- The journey to resolution takes time and has many ups and downs.
- Resolved or not, eventually you may feel that there was a purpose or some positives that arose from your baby's death.
- Whether your grief is resolved or unresolved, anniversary reactions are normal, even years after your baby's death.
- Even in resolution you may wonder about what your child would have been like and what might have been.
- If you feel stuck, counseling may help you move to a more comfortable place with your grief.

# 8

# The Effects of Your Baby's Death on Your Family

## YOU AND YOUR PARTNER

Most couples notice that their relationship is affected after their baby dies. Some feel closer and draw together in sorrow. In the process, they learn more about each other's sensitivities and strengths, and their intimacy and mutual support may be enhanced.

Other couples pull apart and withdraw into blame, displaced anger and misunderstandings. For some, this tragedy becomes a catalyst that breaks up an already troubled relationship. For many couples, a baby's death drives a needless wedge into an otherwise healthy partnership.

As a couple, you may alternate between intimacy and isolation. This may be the first tragedy you've faced together, and you may discover new ways of being there for each other. But sometimes the stress of grieving can make you so needy individually that it can be difficult to support each other. Many of the grieving emotions, such as anger and depression, make it even more of a challenge to be supportive. Often you will grieve very differently from each other, making it hard for you to empathize or accept each other's feelings.

There are things you can do to make sure your relationship survives. Remember that before you were parents, you were friends and lovers. Care about your partner, care about what he or she is feeling, care about what he or she needs. In addition to caring, *communication, acceptance* and *reassurance* are the ingredients that can help a relationship survive.

### COMMUNICATION
Communication in a relationship is normally challenging, and after

a baby dies, the stress of grieving can add tension to your relationship. Misunderstandings flair up easily. You may hesitate sharing your thoughts and feelings about the baby, for fear of burdening each other. It takes energy to communicate, and you may wish your partner could just read your mind or understand you with minimum effort. You may find it difficult to cope with your partner's emotions because you are struggling with your own.

Couples who share thoughts and feelings, however, offer each other valuable support. In particular, a father who talks about the baby and his emotions is a source of comfort to the mother because this lets her know she is not the only one who grieves for her baby. Although it may appear that he is making the mother sad, the father is really inviting her to share the grieving feelings she already has. Sharing feelings reduces the parents' isolation and can help both of them cope better.

Even if you have difficulty expressing your feelings, you can be supportive by listening and allowing your partner to express his or her feelings. Knowing that someone is there to listen and hold you when you cry can be a tremendous support.

> I never felt like I was burdening him with my tears. I needed to talk about it and I needed to cry about it, and he never left me feeling like he didn't want to hear it. Other people tire of hearing your problems, but he never gave me that feeling. He always was willing to listen no matter how many times he heard it.
>
> —Sarah

Many bereaved mothers report that a mutual willingness to listen and an open attitude become invaluable qualities in their relationship. Mourning a baby's death is a shared trauma. Talking about it does not add to the burden, it lessens the pain. By being available, listening and sharing feelings, parents can enhance each other's coping and strengthen their intimacy.

## ACCEPTING YOUR DIFFERENCES

Parents are often dismayed to discover that they grieve differently. Distinct styles can be attributed to normal variations in personality, philosophy, coping style and, in the case of women, postpartum hormonal changes.

Mothers and fathers also grieve differently because they usually feel different levels of bonding to the baby. During pregnancy, the mother usually feels a closer connection with the baby. For the father, the baby is much more abstract until birth. If the baby is miscarried early in the pregnancy, the father usually feels a lesser bond than the mother. As the pregnancy progresses, the father can see the growth occurring, and especially after birth, the fatherly bond deepens. Even so, it is difficult for fathers and mothers to feel the same intense connection with the baby.

> Since this baby was full term, this was the first pregnancy that my husband could identify with. The others were miscarriages, and as each miscarriage occurred, it became the norm to him, I think. He was always concerned about me, but he never ever mentioned the pregnancies. He could never identify with me as to how I felt. All these losses I was on my own, and it was something he could never understand, but with this one, he did.
>
> —Meryl

Because men and women are socialized differently, even if they feel the same sense of connection with the baby, it is natural that they will grieve in different ways. Women are generally expected to be more nurturing and expressive, while men are expected to be strong and unemotional. Although this is not the rule, many couples experience these dynamics: While the mother cries and dwells on her memories of the baby, the father quells his grief and often busies himself in his work. As far as she can see, he is uncaring and has forgotten about the baby. She feels angry at this callousness and isolated as she grieves alone. From the father's view, she will never get over her grief. He impatiently wants her to snap out of it so life can get back to normal.

> My husband says I scare him because I grieve too intensely. We try to find a happy medium where we can talk about it without frightening each other.
>
> —Rosemary

Unfortunately, while mothers are allowed to be emotional,

grieving fathers often feel inhibited by our culture's expectations. "Real men" aren't supposed to cry. Some fathers need to visit their baby's grave in order to feel free enough to shed tears. Fathers may also find it difficult to verbalize their thoughts and feelings. As John says, "For me it just seemed so hopeless to talk about. I couldn't find the words, so why try? There was no handle—it's just a nonverbal hurt."

Isolation for fathers can be tremendous because everyone focuses on the mother, as if he is unaffected. He feels left out when friends and relatives inquire only about the mother's condition. He flinches when others compliment his ability to hold up, because inside he feels so torn down. He may be expected to return to work without any drop in productivity. He may not have male friends who can listen to him talk about his feelings. Francisco notes, "I feel emotionally isolated from my male friends, in contrast to my wife whose female friends talk about this stuff so freely."

Another common dynamic in couples is grieving alternately. If they both fall apart, who would keep everything else together? Somebody has to go back to work, the bills still need to be paid, the pantry needs to be stocked, the other children need care; life does go on. When one of the partners is having an especially hard time, the other often puts grief aside. Sometimes couples switch off daily, sometimes weekly or monthly. Other couples don't switch until a year or so after the baby dies.

> At first, I never saw him cry. I'd talk and talk about the baby and he'd hold me and I'd ask him, "Why don't you cry?" and he'd say, "Well, it's over with, he's dead, what's crying going to do?" And finally one night about three or four months after, he cried and then I was better. I could be strong for him. I just held him and let him cry. It was a big relief to see that, gee, he does care, he is human, because I couldn't figure out why I was so depressed and crying when he was handling it just fine, which he really wasn't.
>
> —Desi

> In one sense it has drawn us closer, but we've been so focused on self-survival that we've grown apart. He

denied his grief for quite a while and wanted me to move on. Then it hit him hard a year later.

—Holly

If you can understand where these differences come from, you may feel less threatened by them. Acceptance is also easier if you remember there are no right or wrong ways to grieve, and no two people grieve alike. What's important is finding what's right for you.

It is also important to avoid judging each other, for instance: "Since he feels this way, he must not care much about the baby" or "She will never get over this if she keeps feeling that way." By simply accepting your partner's feelings, you are acknowledging that he or she is entitled to his or her feelings, just as you are entitled to yours. Remember, accepting another's feelings doesn't negate your own. You may not share your partner's feelings; you may not always understand them. You may even feel angry or disappointed at your partner's reactions. But by accepting each other's silences and tears without judging or placing blame, you encourage nonthreatening communication. You also provide the kind of support and understanding so necessary to promote healing and to enhance your relationship.

Attending a support group may help you to understand your feelings and open lines of communication. By listening to other parents, you can feel reassured that both you and your partner are reacting normally to your loss. By listening to each other share thoughts and emotions in a group, you can get insights about yourself, your partner or your relationship. You may be able to start a healthy dialogue on your feelings about the baby and your grief.

For instance, Carolyn remembers the time her husband casually mentioned to the group that he thought about their daughter Rachel while he painted the house. Although to an observer this may seem unremarkable, he had never told Carolyn about this, and she found it comforting and reassuring to discover that he did think about the baby.

I felt like my husband should be grieving and showing his grief exactly the same way that I was. That if he were grieving, that it would somehow lighten my load. When I heard another parent in group say these same things, then

> I started realizing it was just absurd. I was expecting him
> to do the work for me and angry at him for not being an
> identical twin.
>
> —Liza

## REASSURANCE

Before the baby died, your relationship may have been open and sharing, relatively effortless. Unfortunately, grieving can create chasms that can easily widen, and you may fear that your partner will abandon you. Ironically, these concerns can make you withdraw even more as you try to protect yourself from the hurt. Or you may try to protect yourself with blame and anger, using these emotions to push your partner away. Unconsciously you may operate on the principle "I'll quit before I'm fired" or "I'll leave you before you can leave me!"

> We had mostly grieved at a similar rate and style for the
> first couple of months, and then it seemed as though I felt
> a lot more alone. Kent was handling it in his own way
> and I was handling it in my own way, and it was becom-
> ing a problem in the relationship.
>
> —Jessie

> I expected John to be the one person I could hang on to in
> the storm. But through the thick of it, we were both
> staggering under our own burdens and we couldn't
> possibly pick up another pound. As a result, we each
> staggered alone for a while.
>
> —Claudia

As difficult and sometimes frightening as it is to risk rejection, you need to build bridges, not walls. Reassuring each other of your love and devotion can guard against fears of losing each other. It is reasonable to ask your partner if she still cares about you or to ask if he blames you. In turn, you can reassure your partner that you still love her or that you don't blame him for your baby's death. You both need to be sensitive to each other's needs for this kind of reassurance.

> It really helped that my husband kept telling me that I
> was important and kept telling me that we were there

before the baby and we would still be there after the baby
and that kind of thing, always telling me how much he
cared for me.

—Bryn

We kept hearing that everybody who said they'd lost a
baby said they split up and we thought, "Oh, we can't do
that! We've lost something already." So we got a lot
closer.

—Martina

## SEX AND INTIMACY

For some couples, sex provides the intimacy and reassurance they
need from each other. However, for many couples sex becomes a
tension point. When a couple is drained emotionally and physically,
when they feel depressed or angry, or when communication breaks
down, sex may be the last thing they desire. For many parents, the link
between sex and conception is painfully obvious. For others, the
association between sex and affection makes them feel hurt by their
partner's lack of desire.

Negotiating your sexual relationship requires more communication, acceptance and reassurance. Be sensitive to your own and
each other's emotional needs during this stressful time. By talking,
listening and holding each other, you can maintain feelings of
affection and intimacy without the pressures of intercourse. You can
find comfort in spending quality time together, including dinner for
two, going for long walks and sharing other activities you enjoy. In
time, as your grief becomes more manageable, your sexual relationship
can become more comfortable.

## CAN OUR RELATIONSHIP SURVIVE?

Many couples experience stress after their baby dies, but their
marriage survives. Sophie, Rose, Bess and Clara talk about the
difficulties they encountered.

The first month or so after Stephanie died, Cal was very
supportive and did as much as he could to help me
physically as well as emotionally. But there was some
point after a month or so—maybe he had deferred some

of his grieving because he was so busy taking care of me—where he kind of lost his patience and there was a lot of tension between the two of us. We got some counseling at that point. And it went through my head that events like this either really cement a marriage or blow it out of the water entirely: "Which one are we going to do?" So then I'd get scared that my marriage was also falling apart, but then I began to understand that Cal was dealing with his own grieving and his own stress. He'd been so superattentive to me that he finally was worn out and couldn't do it anymore.

—Sophie

I hated my husband. I felt like he wasn't sympathetic and he wasn't grieving like I thought he should be. I didn't really see him for about six months because he was trying to bury himself by keeping busy, school and work, thirteen hours a day.

—Rose

We never really blamed each other for what happened, but there was just stress. There was so much unhappiness for having lost the baby that I think we took it out on each other. Then he, trying to handle grief his way, would go elsewhere sometimes, and that was very, very difficult. I became very dependent on him and then when he wasn't there, it hurt me more and I became very angry with him. I remember that spring I asked him to move out of the house, and then we got back together and went to counseling.

—Bess

Right after the baby died, there was this honeymoon period where we felt, "We're alive, I love you so much, we'll try again soon," and then you start drifting apart into your own grief and grieving so differently, and that incredible closeness goes away. But then we came back together eventually.

—Clara

For some couples the stress may break apart an already floundering relationship or create problems that seem too big to overcome. Poor communication habits that existed before the pregnancy may flare up and ignite smoldering longstanding issues such as sex, money and relatives. Maria recalls, "After Matthew died, we simply stopped talking and we had nothing in common anymore. We lost each other." Anya remembers how she and her husband drifted apart: "My husband never talked about her, ever. He never showed his feelings, never held her, did not want pictures, never cried."

> As soon as we got home he said the cruelest words a person could say: "If you hadn't gone skiing, we'd have a healthy child." I felt so guilty. I thought I'd murdered my own baby because I'd gone skiing. That was the beginning of the end of our marriage.
>
> —Lena

If you are both determined that your relationship will survive this tragedy, it probably will. Many couples benefit from counseling. A therapist can help you understand why you are withdrawing or quarreling and help you sort out the underlying fears and tensions. Keeping your relationship going is hard work, but the payoffs of strengthened communication and deeper commitment can make the struggle worthwhile. Faith advises marriage counseling for anyone having trouble: "It saved my marriage. And after my baby died, the last thing I needed was a divorce, to lose my husband too!"

Many couples are reassured by the fact that they came through this experience feeling closer than ever. You may have opened up new lines of communication or discovered things about each other that enhance your intimacy or commitment. You may even realize a sense of accomplishment—if your relationship can survive this, it can survive anything.

> It was wonderful for our relationship. It's an awful thing to say, but it's really true. It brought us so much closer together and we've managed to keep close. It was a real binding kind of thing, finding strengths we didn't know each other had.
>
> —Sarah

# YOUR PARENTS— YOUR BABY'S GRANDPARENTS

Not only do I grieve the death of my grandson, I grieve
for my daughter. I don't want her to have any pain
because she's *my* baby, and I can't make it better.

—Pearl

Many grandparents endure a double sorrow. They grieve for the
grandchild who will never grow up and they grieve for you, their
child, who suffers the death of a baby. Your parents may feel very
helpless because they cannot lessen your suffering. They may feel the
same anger that you experience and may want to blame someone for
their grandchild's death. If they have ever lost children of their own,
they may relive that pain now. In any case, you may feel as though you
have to protect them from your despair.

My mother cares so much, I feel like I can't give her a
whole lot of my problem. ... She'll just feel so awful
herself. It's not that I couldn't say anything to her, but I
just thought, "Why?" It won't help me, it won't help her
and I'll feel like I have to take care of her.

—Meryl

It's easier to talk to somebody who's unrelated because relatives have so much emotion themselves. I felt I had to protect them, you know; my mom lost a grandchild. We didn't
talk about it that much. They were there, but no one really
talked because we didn't know what to say to each other.

—Erin

At a time when you want to depend on your parents for
emotional support, they may not be able to give it for one reason or
another. Some simply do not understand the grieving process that you
must go through. Others may have lost babies of their own, but if they
were not encouraged or allowed to grieve, acknowledging your grief
would require them to examine their own. For many, that's too painful.
Instead, they may try to belittle your baby's importance in order to
protect themselves from their own sadness, and you from yours.

Even more difficult, some grandparents may not readily recognize the baby as a grandchild, particularly if there are other grandchildren. You may feel very hurt when they make comments that appear to discount your baby's life, or when they don't say anything.

> My mother came in the hospital room and was trying to
> be real cheerful and happy and perk me up and make me
> feel better. She didn't really let down too much around
> me. She did with my sister. With me she was trying to be
> the "good mommy" and that kind of stuff. I felt like she
> didn't have to do that. I cried when anybody came into
> my room, and they did too, and she didn't need to be
> so ... . The crying made me feel better!
>
> —Hannah

> My mother-in-law was furious that we sent out an-
> nouncements of our baby's death. She said, "It wasn't
> even a baby you lost." It turns out she had a miscarriage
> but never grieved and was told, "Just have another baby
> and forget it."
>
> —Clara

> I wish that my mother could talk about David more. She
> could say, "I know it's that time of year and I'm thinking
> about him too," but she can't. My husband and I are
> pretty much the only ones who ever think that February is
> difficult. Sometimes I wish someone would acknowledge
> that he existed.
>
> —Bess

When your parents aren't supportive, avoid telling them what they are doing wrong—criticism is rarely productive. Instead, make suggestions for what they can do to help. You may be afraid to tell them what you need for fear they won't respond, and then you'll be even more disappointed. However, you have a right to at least try. If it is difficult to talk to them, you could write a letter or send a photocopy of a chapter or article on supporting bereaved parents. If they cannot be supportive, focus on friends or other family members who can be there for you.

Sometimes grandparents become more supportive if they are included in acknowledging the baby's life. Show them your mementos and any pictures you have. Invite them to the funeral or send a formal announcement. Ask them to memorialize your baby in their own way, perhaps by making a donation, planting a tree, lighting a candle or including the baby in their prayers. Point out that your grief will last a long time and that you'd appreciate their sensitivity. You may also decide to forgive any misguided efforts on their part because you know they mean well.

Some grandparents are able to be supportive without much prompting. Your parents may be educated about grief or may naturally react sensitively and compassionately to your needs. Or they may be responsive to your suggestions.

> My mom thought of things like getting him an outfit, donating my extra milk to the La Leche League. That was very helpful, being able to do what I could as far as the mothering role I wanted to be in at that time.
>
> —Kara

# OTHER CHILDREN IN THE FAMILY

How the other children in the family respond to the death of their baby sibling will depend on several factors, including:

- their level of understanding about death
- their relationship with the baby
- their reaction to the parents' grief
- the support and reassurance they receive

## EXPLAINING DEATH TO CHILDREN

In the past, discussing death with children was considered insensitive and unnecessary. Parents avoided talking about death to spare children from sadness. They often answered questions with misinformation to protect the children's innocence. However, by telling children stories such as "Grandma went on a long trip" or "Spot went to sleep and won't be waking up again," their well-intentioned remarks only added elements of fear, rejection or anger to the sense of loss. A child who is told, "Grandma went on a long trip" may wonder, "Why did Grandma leave me without saying goodbye and why can't I visit her? Doesn't she want to see me?" A child who is told, "Spot went to sleep" may worry, "If I go to sleep, will I be able to wake up?" A child who is told, "Billy is with God" or "God needed another angel" may be fearful or angry toward a God who takes people away forever. In these attempts to spare children the pain of grief, parents may unwittingly intensify disturbed feelings.

Nowadays, most parents recognize that children can cope better when they are informed. There are no perfect words to explain death to children. The words you use however, should be honest, informative and age-appropriate. When your children ask questions or make confusing or false statements about death, take the cue and answer, clarify and reassure them. You will not overwhelm your children if you take into account their ability to comprehend and their need for information and reassurance. If you feel comfortable talking about death, then they will feel comfortable asking you questions. For parents who feel uncomfortable, reading stories together about a child coping with death and grief can open up discussion. (See Bibliography, "Books for Parents and Children.")

Children's ability to understand death depends on their level of intellectual development—the way they view the world and relationships between things and events. Until adolescence, many children need to experience and think about things in tangible ways. But death is not tangible. It is not something they can be for a little while to see what it's like. It's not something they can do to see how it works and it's not a place they can visit to see how it looks. As a result, young children cannot understand death the way adults do—that death is when the body is no longer alive, that it is irreversible and depending on beliefs, the person either ceases to exist, the spirit goes to heaven or to another plane of existence, or the person goes on to be reincarnated as another living being.

Most children acquire an inaccurate understanding of death, but this is not necessarily a problem. They may simply have a unique way of looking at it, a way that causes them no concern. Other children may have some misconceptions about death that frighten them. Rather than focusing on how accurately your children understand death, try to address any concerns or fears they may have. (See "Providing the Support and Reassurance Your Children Need" later in this chapter.)

## ATTENDING THE FUNERAL AND
## OTHER RITUALS OF MOURNING

In the past, many parents felt that siblings should be spared from attending the baby's funeral or graveside services. However, children who are not allowed to participate in these rituals may feel excluded from the family at a time when they need to be surrounded by loved ones. Being a part of the family, seeing how others grieve and hearing others talk lovingly about the baby are comforting and help them sort out their feelings about the death. They may also gain understanding about where and how the dead are buried or ashes are spread, instead of being left to think about scenes from cartoons or horror films about skeletons rising from dusty, crumbling graveyards. If you can explain to them what the baby's funeral or service will be like, you may be able to encourage them to go. You may be able to encourage them to attend some family gatherings and to forgo others. It is better to err on the side of allowing children to be a part of rituals and family gatherings, rather than excluding them.

## UNDERSTANDING YOUR CHILDREN'S SENSE OF LOSS

If your children knew there was a baby but the baby never came home, they may wonder where the baby went. But children vary widely as to how much they look forward to a new baby. Unlike parents and older children, many younger children cannot form an imaginary bond with the baby. Without emotional investment in the idea of having a new baby/sibling/companion/rival/roommate, very young children will not grieve the death of this invisible baby because there is no loss felt.

If your children looked forward to playing with or helping you with the baby, they may feel deeply disappointed. If your baby lived for several months and your children had time to develop a bond with the baby, they may grieve. Even so, your children do not share the same anticipation or fantasies as you and will not grieve as intensely. In fact, your children may have harbored some resentment or jealousy as they watched you fuss over the baby or the nursery. Your children's apparent lack of concern for the baby after a few days may strike you as callous. But if allowed and encouraged, your children will grieve according to the unique sense of loss they feel.

If you suffered a miscarriage, your children may not have even known that you were pregnant, especially if they are young. Even so, your children will respond to the family disequilibrium caused by the baby's death. The disruption of familiar routines and the changes in you—from playful, responsive and easygoing to sad, withdrawn and irritable—can be very distressing to young children. Children are naturally egocentric and easily assume that they are the cause of your anger or despair. Even if you try to hide your feelings, children are very perceptive and may become more confused and anxious by your reticence.

## PROVIDING THE SUPPORT AND REASSURANCE YOUR CHILDREN NEED

From infancy through adolescence, children often show their grief, confusion or anxiety by changes in their behavior. If your children are upset you may notice:

- regression in abilities, including motor skills, toileting, talking, schoolwork
- regression into infantile behaviors such as baby talk, chewing on toys
- increased separation anxiety, clinging, not letting you out of sight, not wanting to go to school
- disrupted sleep or appetite, increased night waking
- irritability, obstinacy or aggression, including fretfulness, tantrums, biting
- withdrawal from you or others, turning away
- decreased adaptability, including low tolerance for changes in routine, new foods, contact with other people, even if familiar

Your children's behavior and questions are a barometer of their feelings and how they are coping. Whenever your children are acting out, there is an underlying problem that needs to be addressed. Common underlying concerns around death and grief include:

- fears of sleep or of illness
- concerns about dead bodies
- fears of separation or of abandonment

In addition, children may act out when they are having difficulty coping with feelings, particularly anger and guilt. By understanding the concerns and issues your children may be wrestling with, you will be in a better position to offer support. By dealing with the underlying problem, you can help your children find real solutions that diminish the need to act out.

### Fears of Sleep or of Illness

Particularly if your children hear people equating death with sleep, or if they have a chance to see the baby after death, they may conclude that death is similar to sleep. There are several signs that your children may be confusing death and sleep.

- They are restless at naptime or bedtime.
- They wake up in the night and can't get back to sleep.
- They ask you why the baby won't wake up.

To reassure your children, you can explain that death and sleep are totally different, that sleep is necessary for a healthy body, and that your body stays alive when you sleep, and then you wake up. In death, the heart and breathing stop, and then the body dies and can't become alive again. Your children may have difficulty understanding it all, but the message that sleep and death are totally different should sink in.

If your baby died from an infection or other illness, your children may equate sickness with impending death. The following are indications that your children may be worried about illness.

- They ask many or repetitive questions about illness, disease, germs, health.
- They ask many or repetitive questions about why the baby died.
- They are concerned about getting sick or being around sick people.
- They are worried that you will get sick.

Give your children as much information as they need about the baby's illness or birth defects. Emphasize the difference between weak, little babies and big, strong, healthy kids like them and grownups like you.

Luke asked tons of questions about what made his
brother die. I think he was worried that the same fate
might befall him. So I assured him that babies aren't as
strong as older kids, so he decided that for a baby to
survive the first year, to make it "past zero" to 1, was
very difficult, but that since he was 4, he was out of
danger. He would reassure himself by saying, "It's hard to
make it past zero."

—Cathryn

### Concerns about Dead Bodies

If children resist attending the funeral or graveside service, or if
they seem preoccupied with dead bodies, burial, cremation, or
afterlife, it is important to help them sort out their fears. For example,
are they concerned about the baby suffering? Are they afraid the body
may burst out of the casket? Do they worry about skeletons and
ghosts? Your children may acquire scary ideas about death from
movies, television, comic books or friends; children are prone to
misinterpreting what they see and hear, of confusing fantasy with
reality.

You can reassure your children by answering questions honestly,
giving whatever details they require. Let their questions be your guide
and keep in mind children's need for reassurance that death is a
natural end of life and a quiet, peaceful existence. Some children are
satisfied with the idea that the physical body stays in the earth or turns
to ashes while the spirit goes to a peaceful place. Your own personal
beliefs can provide a comforting framework for your children, even
if the abstract idea of "spirits" is hard to grasp. For younger children
struggling with the concept of death, emphasize that a dead body
cannot move or feel anything, including loneliness or pain. Talking
to your children about these stark realities may be difficult and
sorrowful but you may also benefit from these reassuring reminders
that your baby is not suffering.

### Fears of Separation or of Abandonment

When a new baby arrives, most children have trouble dealing
with this separation from mother and all the attention given to the
baby. When a baby dies, siblings have to deal with the physical
separation *and* a change in both of their parents. Children may

wonder, "If the baby can go away, then what's to prevent Mommy and Daddy from going away?"

During this difficult time, your children need reassurance that you can still take care of them, that you still love them, and that eventually you will feel better. You are your children's main source of emotional support, and they need you to be there.

There are several clues that your children are having fears of separation or abandonment.

- They regress into infantile behaviors such as baby talk, tantrums, wetting.
- They regress in abilities such as speech, toileting, play, schoolwork.
- They are more prone to separation anxiety, dependence, clinginess, fears.
- They are more prone to irritability, obstinacy, angry outbursts, demanding behavior.
- They withdraw, turn away.

Regression into infantile behavior may be a way of trying to regain the safe feelings of earlier times, when you took care of so many of your children's needs. If your children feel neglected, they may make bids for your attention by becoming more annoying, fearful or clingy. Many children can also become more aggressive, angry or withdrawn. Be alert to any of these signals that your children need more reassurance and attention from you. Even when your children are irritable, a hug or a gentle reminder that you love them may be soothing. With your comfort and empathy, they will regain confidence and security sooner than if you ignore these bids for attention or insist that they "act their age" and be as independent as they were before the baby died.

If your children exhibit any of these behaviors when you leave them with other caregivers, they may need extra assurance that you will return. Also beware of your own anxieties. If you are worried about her safety or care in your absence, she may pick up on this and not want you to leave. This unwitting, inadvertent collusion is common between parents and children.

When their world has turned upside down, some children have an increased need to feel in control. They may still have fears of abandonment, but instead of clinging, they assert their preferences and ideas in order to gain some feelings of competence and mastery. Obstinacy and tantrums are common. If you notice that you and your children are getting into power struggles, try offering more choices and letting your children be in charge of some things. At the same time, continue to meet your children's needs for attention and dependence. Even if your children seem self-reliant, they still need reassurance that you are available.

Children also need reassurance that they are not the cause of their parents' distress. When you feel sad or upset about the baby, it is important for you to be open about it and to assure your children that your feelings are due to your grief over the baby's death.

Unfortunately, when you are in the depths of grief, it can be very difficult to be a responsive parent. It is hard enough to deal with your own grief let alone the day-to-day needs of your children. Ultimately, by taking care of your own emotional needs, you will be able to reinvest in nurturing your children. So, when parenting becomes overwhelming or draining, rely on your partner (or other adults your children enjoy) to take up the slack. Or find someone to help you with the mundane chores so you can be available to your children at critical times. Try to make sure your children don't feel abandoned.

> After William died, I found it very difficult to be a
> nurturing mother to my girls. I was grieving so much that
> I had nothing left for them. I felt guilty about that, like I
> wasn't a good mother, but I pretty much left their care to
> my husband for the first couple months. And then,
> eventually, as I felt better, I was able to be an attentive
> mother again.
>
> —Edie

### HELPING YOUR CHILDREN EXPRESS FEELINGS

Allow your children to vent their feelings, including fear, anxiety, sadness, anger, guilt or relief. You can help your children cope by encouraging them to express their feelings—by drawing pictures, writing stories, dictating letters or playing out emotions in dramatic scenes with toys. It may help if you can share some of your feelings and engage in a dialogue. Reading stories about death and grief can help your children clarify feelings. By allowing your children to express feelings, you help them identify and cope with them in constructive, healthy ways.

When a promised baby sibling doesn't materialize, children may feel angry toward their parents. Young children tend to see their parents as all-powerful. If you promise a baby, you should be able to bring one home. Your children may reason that you caused the baby's death or somehow sabotaged this promise. They may even take it personally, assuming that you did this to disappoint or aggravate them.

Children need answers as much as adults do. If you can explain that the baby's death was a cruel twist of nature, that no one is to blame, that you are angry too, you can help your children direct their anger away from you. You can help your children express their anger and disappointment by encouraging them to draw pictures, talk about their feelings, dictate a letter to God or Mother Nature or pound on pillows. (See chapter 6 for more on expressing anger.)

> We kept telling our 6-year-old son that it was OK to be angry, but then when he would get mad, we'd tell him to stop it. So, finally, he regressed to wetting his pants and biting, and I realized that not only did I need to allow him to express anger, but I needed to give *myself* permission to express anger.
>
> —Amy

Children are naturally egocentric. They often believe that things happen because their actions, thoughts or wishes are powerful enough to cause things to happen. This egocentric thinking may make your children feel responsible for the baby's death. Before the death they may have felt competitive or resentful that the new baby would get all the attention. Your children may have wished that the baby would never be born, or would go away forever. When the baby dies, your children may worry that their thoughts were indeed powerful enough to cause the baby to go away forever. They may feel horribly guilty and yet be unable to admit it.

This self-centered thinking may also lead your children to feel responsible for your grief. When you are feeling mad, your children may naturally assume that they did something bad to cause your anger. If you are sad, your children may think that they did something to disappoint you. To compound this, your children may worry that you are upset because you have figured out that their wishes caused the baby to die.

To assuage any feelings of responsibility for the baby's death, your children can benefit from repeated explanations of the possible or definite physiological reasons for your baby's death. In addition, your children need your assurances that nobody is to blame, that thoughts or wishes or unrelated actions cannot make bad things happen.

Let your children know that they are not responsible for your grief. Be open about your feelings of grief and explain that you are upset because you miss the baby. Even if you try to hide your feelings, children are very perceptive, and your underlying feelings will not escape their notice. You needn't share your private, overwhelming emotions with them, but if you can talk about your feelings and explain why you cry, you can reduce their confusion or anxiety. The more information they have, the better they will feel. They need to know that you aren't upset with them, and that they aren't to blame. Your children will also learn about loss and grief and may even see your sadness as assurance that if they died, you would grieve for them too.

Your children may have other fears and worries about death not covered here. If you become concerned by any behavior, it may be helpful to talk with a family counselor who is knowledgeable about how grief affects families. The counselor can help you figure out what your children need to get through this family crisis.

Children react to death and grief according to their level of maturity. It can be helpful for parents to understand the special needs of toddlers, young children, older children and adolescents. The age ranges are guidelines only, as your children may very well have special needs described under any of the age groups.

## TODDLERS—UNDER 3 YEARS

It is difficult to know how much children under age 3 understand about the baby in Mommy's tummy or what it means when Mommy and Daddy come back from the hospital without the baby. Nevertheless, toddlers are especially affected by family disequilibrium after a baby's death. Whether your toddler grieves or not, he or she will notice the changes in your behavior. You can help your toddler cope by trying to be as consistently nurturing and patient as possible. You may feel so grateful to have a little one at home, but even so, nurturing and patience can be difficult when you are grieving. Try bringing a friend, relative or favorite babysitter into your home to help you with the mundane tasks so that you have more energy to meet your toddler's needs.

> Having Lisa made me feel very much better. If I had had a miscarriage before having her, I probably would have thought I'll never have a baby. But I had one at home to come home to. I was so thankful to have her. I felt empty inside, but I didn't feel like I was empty-handed.
>
> —Jane

If you have a surviving twin, you may be grateful to have a baby, but you still need to grieve. Anya recalls, "That made it harder in some ways. Because I had Kim to focus on, I put off working through some of my feelings about Rachel, so I think it dragged out for a longer period of time." Even in infancy, your baby will notice your grief and preoccupation. Your baby needs nurturing, social interaction and stimulation in order to thrive. You may want to enlist the help of another consistent caregiver—your partner, a friend or a relative. This assistance can be a nurturing support to both you and your baby.

Although it can be challenging to grieve for one baby while trying to nurture another, having a surviving twin can make things easier for you in other ways. As Anya says, "I don't know what it's like to lose a baby and not have another baby there too. I did have a baby to hold. I've never had a pregnancy and nothing to show for it."

### YOUNG CHILDREN—2 TO 7 YEARS

Many young children think of death as life under different circumstances. People don't simply disappear. They must have gone somewhere else, and surely they will return, or at least you can retrieve them from wherever it is they have gone. To young children, death may be reversible, and some children may associate it with sleep. You may be barraged with questions like "When is the baby coming back?" or "Can we go get the baby from the hospital now?" or "When will the baby wake up?" You need to patiently explain that being dead means the baby won't come back, that the baby's body cannot move or breathe anymore. In attempts to understand what you mean, your children may raise new concerns such as "Where is the baby?" or "Why can't we go there?" or "Why did the baby die?" or "Am I going to die?" or "Are you going to die?" Your children may seem obsessed with playing out scenes of death or making up songs about babies dying. While this behavior may seem morbid or even maddening to you, this is your children's way of trying to master the meaning of your baby's death.

Even if you carefully explain the cause of death in physiological terms or the fact that the body is buried but the spirit goes to a higher plane, it is important to remember that young children cannot always interpret these explanations correctly. Because they are unable to grasp abstract concepts, children this age are mystified by death and may worry about whatever they cannot understand. They think about death in concrete, egocentric or magical ways, and sometimes these can provoke anxiety. If you have children this age, it is especially important to be aware of the fears that children commonly have about death so that you can reassure them.

Answer questions honestly, in terms your children can both understand and cope with. You might try saying, "Dead means we can't see the baby again." If your children are not frightened by the idea of a body failing, you can try saying, "The baby died because his (or her) body couldn't stay alive and breathe." You can go into as much detail as your children's curiosity requires. However you explain it, make sure your children feel reassured and know that you won't disappear next, or that their body is not likely to fail in the same way, without warning.

> I tried to explain to Kristen [age 28 months] about how the body stops working, but she yelled, "No, no, no." Maybe that was too much for her to handle, so we just left it that "died" means we can't see them anymore and that I wasn't going anywhere.
>
> —Terri

## OLDER CHILDREN—6 TO 12 YEARS

Most older children are curious about death. They are concerned with rituals, where the body goes, where the spirit goes. They may still consider themselves somehow responsible for the baby's death.

> It was really hard on my 10-year-old daughter. She had
> been wanting a brother or sister, but then when I was
> pregnant she said, "I don't want a brother; they're mean."
> So when Gregory died, she blamed it on herself. So next
> time I was pregnant, she said, "I don't care what—if you
> have a monkey, Mom, that's fine."
>
> —Martina

Children this age are often more able to hide their feelings because they want to maintain control or seem grown up. If you hide your feelings, they may take that cue from you. If you are more open and share some of your feelings, this may encourage them to vent their own.

## ADOLESCENTS—OVER 10 YEARS

Adolescents usually have sophisticated ideas about death, but may still have many questions and concerns about the physiological and spiritual aspects of death. They may feel some embarrassment about pregnancy and sexuality and perhaps guilt about any feelings of resentment toward the baby. Adolescents can seem so grown up, yet it is important to remember that they are naturally self-centered and immature and may say cruel or insensitive things. Adolescents can benefit greatly from your honesty and sharing feelings, as well as your acceptance of their feelings.

## AS YOUR CHILDREN GROW

As time goes on, children may seem to have recovered from the baby's death, but memories of one kind or another may surface from time to time. As children grow older, they become more sophisticated in their ability to understand death, and the death of a younger sibling may take on new meaning. For a 3-year-old girl whose baby brother died, the typical questions are: "When is the baby coming back?" and "Where did he go?" and "Why can't we see him?" When this girl is older, she may ask more detailed questions concerning the physical and spiritual nature of death, and she may be concerned about the rituals of burial. As an adolescent, she may have thoughts and questions about how her life might have been different if her brother had survived. As children acquire new understanding about death and the meaning of the loss of a sibling, they need to have continuing support and information from their parents.

## POINTS TO REMEMBER

- As a couple you may notice that your baby's death affects your relationship—sometimes for better, sometimes for worse.
- Key ingredients to help your relationship survive this tragedy include caring, communication, acceptance and reassurance.
- Grandparents often carry a double sorrow as they grieve for their grandchild and for you, their own child.
- Many grandparents have difficulty supporting their grieving children. It may help to include them as much as possible in affirming and memorializing your baby.
- Children grieve according to the loss they feel. Young children, in particular, are primarily affected by your grief and the family imbalance resulting from the baby's death.
- It can be difficult to nurture your other children when you are grieving. Have others help you with the mundane caregiving tasks, so you can be more available to your children.
- Children need information and clarification about death and grief. Otherwise, they can fear death or feel responsible for your sadness or even for the baby's death. By being honest and by sharing some of your feelings, you can help them understand and cope.
- Children often need help expressing their feelings in constructive ways. Try to be a good example; children learn a lot by watching you handle your own feelings.
- Children need reassurance that you are still there to love and take care of them and that you are upset because the baby died, not because of something they have done.

# 9

# Support Networks

## FRIENDS AND RELATIVES

The most supportive friends and relatives are those who recognize that your baby's death is a significant and tragic loss. They try to understand what you are going through, they listen whenever you need to talk and they accept your behavior and your emotions without being uncomfortable or judgmental. Having this kind of support can help you cope with your baby's death. Friends who are able to anticipate the moments that might be particularly painful for you or who can alert others to your sensitivity are always good to have around. Even if you tend to handle things by yourself, you may feel better just knowing that someone else sympathizes and cares.

> My sister and my friend Sally, they were just always there and I could act how I wanted to act, be distracted, things like that. Just to know they were aware of things. Like when we went out to eat, Sally would tell people what happened so they wouldn't come rushing up and say, "Oh, what did you have?" She just did anticipatory stuff that turned out to be real helpful.
>
> —Hannah

As a result of your loss, you may discover the true meaning of friendship, as some friends stand by you through thick and thin. Sadly, some friends won't align themselves with your sorrow, perhaps because of their own discomfort. However, you may be touched by the kindness of casual acquaintances, particularly those who have experienced loss and grief. You may even form long-lasting bonds with these people, who may turn out to be more supportive than old friends.

## WHEN FRIENDS TURN AWAY

> To us she was real, but to others Claire was just "still-born." I think people just brush her off as insignificant.
>
> —Henry

> It surprised me how few people will cry with you. I don't know where this idea of strength comes in, that you're strong if you don't cry.
>
> —Bess

Unfortunately, supportive friends can be few and far between. After your baby dies, you may discover that many friends and relatives do not recognize the importance of this baby or the significance of your loss. They may be supportive at first, but soon wonder why you aren't feeling better. Holly recalls, "There's that period where everybody's very attentive and then they all fade away and people expect you to be better or they don't want to bring it up." In particular, you may sense these attitudes from people who are unfamiliar or uncomfortable with death and grief. You may find your loss more difficult to bear for several reasons.

- People expect you to have minimal grief. ("Aren't you over this yet? Gee, you can always have another one.")
- Rituals—naming, baptism, funeral, memorials—are often considered unnecessary. ("What's the big deal? This really wasn't a baby.")
- You may feel alone in your grief, that you are the only one who cares about this baby. ("Why are you so upset? You never even got attached to that baby.")

## UNSETTLING REMARKS

Most bereaved parents have endured insensitive, rationalistic statements from well-meaning people who are trying to erase their pain. Here is a small sampling, and how it can feel to hear these remarks.

"You're healthy, young. You can always have another baby."
    But you want *this* baby.

"Be thankful that you already have a healthy child."
    But children can't replace each other.

"I know just how you feel. My dog died last summer."
    They presume to know how you feel or belittle your grief by
    making comparisons.

"Your baby is a little angel in heaven."
    But you don't want a little angel. You want a baby in your arms.

"This is nature's way of weeding out the defective ones."
    But why did this have to happen to you and your baby?

"I've known other people who have handled this well, never cried."
    Handling this well means expressing grief, not repressing it.

"You're lucky it happened now instead of six months from now."
    How on earth can your baby's death be "lucky"?!

"At least you know you are fertile."
    It is hardly a comfort to know you can conceive but can't keep
    the baby.

"At least your loss was final. When our house burned down, for
months we kept remembering more things we were missing."
    But you too will always miss your baby and remember what
    might have been as the years go by!

Other unsettling remarks may make light of your baby or your
loss or may aggravate your grief by pointing out others' tragic losses.

I had my share of insensitivity. An elderly neighbor said,
"Isn't that funny, this other lady could have quadruplets
and you couldn't even have one."
                                                        —Bryn

Somebody asked me, "Why did you name him? It was just a miscarriage!"

—Kelly

When the twins were born prematurely, somebody told me, "Well at least you have two extra income tax deductions for this year."

—Anya

A friend told me, "My mother lost a baby and she *never* got over it." I was ready to kick her in the teeth. People say really stupid things to people who are grieving, and I understand why—because they don't know what to say."

—Sophie

Someone said to me, "Don't worry, I know a woman who had thirteen miscarriages before she had a baby." I thought "Oh God. I don't want to hear that!" She was trying to help, but that was not really the right thing to say.

—Peg

While most people have good intentions, there may be some, even relatives, who are abrasive or malicious. Try to remember that these people have problems and push blame or resentment on you as a way of avoiding their own pain. They may make remarks such as "What did you do to deserve this?" Remind yourself that you certainly do not deserve their incrimination for something beyond your control! You need to take care of yourself by avoiding people who cannot be compassionate.

## EDUCATING FRIENDS ABOUT WHAT YOU NEED

This has been a real learning experience for both of us, to find out that all the supposedly comforting things we used to say to our friends who had miscarriages, those are really some of the worst things to say.

—Mark

Even if your friends have good intentions, you may feel isolated and angry because they don't know how to comfort you. Remember, your friends want to be supportive, but like most people they are uninformed about grief and what bereaved parents need. It can be easy for you and even your well-meaning friends to fall into cycles of misunderstanding.

- When friends make unsympathetic remarks, you may conclude that they are minimizing your baby's importance. Perhaps they just want you to feel better and mistakenly believe that they can ease your pain by rationalizing your baby's death.
- Your friends' silence may lead you to believe that they don't want to be burdened with your sorrow. Instead, they may avoid talking about the baby because they think that will protect you from your despair and help you forget.
- While their misguided efforts can appear uncaring, your friends simply may not realize that certain statements sound hurtful or unfeeling to you.
- Your friends may feel helpless because they want to be supportive but aren't sure how. You may believe some of them are belittling your grief, but most likely they are simply uncomfortable around bereaved people.
- When your friends talk about others who have lost babies, you may wonder why they are insensitively deepening your sense of hopelessness. Yet they are only trying to let you know that you aren't alone, that there are others who have survived what you are going through.

Naturally, if you interpret your friends' actions as uncaring, you will feel uncomfortable sharing your emotions with them. Even if you realize they are trying to help, you may find it difficult to tolerate their blunders when you are feeling so vulnerable and sensitive. If they avoid the subject, you may feel awkward or afraid to talk about your baby. You may think you have to protect *them* by not bringing it up, especially around friends who are pregnant or have babies, or during celebrations or the holiday season. It is a challenge to confront friends or suggest what you need when you are feeling so sad and helpless.

You feel so insecure you don't feel like you've got a right
to stand up and say, "You know, that's really inappropriate. How dare you say something like that!" I wanted to
wear a shirt that said "Please Be Nice to Me."

—Bryn

With some of our friends who were clearly uncomfortable
with this event in our lives, I remember feeling isolated.
Initially they supported me, but with that really bad
period of depression I was getting subtle—and not so
subtle—hints from people that it was time to get on with
things, and I didn't feel *ready* to get on with things. I
think I only heard that from people who hadn't experienced any kind of death of anyone close. Mostly I avoided
people who made me feel that way.

—Jessie

A lot of friends were afraid to talk to me for fear they
would upset me. I could've talked to any of them, but
they really didn't understand and I didn't want to depress
them. I probably tried to hide it more when I was around
them, act like I was handling it.

—Rayleen

Friends backed off, and I understand that now. It was too
close to home, especially for people that had little children. They acted as if, "I don't even want to *think* that
*my* baby could die." So when this happened to me, it
made it real to them, they backed off and they didn't
come around for a while.

—Cindy

It is common for bereaved parents and their friends to disengage
from each other. Parents often retreat if they sense that their grief is
an imposition, and then they notice their friends back off even
further. An irony about grief is that when you withdraw, you may
need people's support more than ever, but people sense your withdrawal and leave you alone. If you feel as though your friends and
family have backed off, remember, they take cues from you. Don't fall

into thinking, "If they really loved me they would know what I need." They can't read your mind. *Tell* them how miserable you really are and how much you need to talk about the baby. Instead of waiting for them to bring it up, you can initiate conversations about how painful this is and how much you miss your baby.

Even though it can be difficult, you do have the right to let people know what helps and what doesn't. You can give them something to read (including this book), write them a letter or tell them in person. It takes energy and courage to confront people, but sometimes that is the only way they will know how to support you. Friends and relatives are usually grateful to know what you need. They truly want to help, and they appreciate your guidance. Surround yourself with people who can be responsive and compassionate.

> It was about three to four months until I saw my family, and they obviously didn't want to bring it up and it was never really discussed. Looking back, that's something I would do differently. Now I'd probably say, "Hey, look, I want to talk about this."
>
> —Dara

> I say to my friends, "I feel like everybody is tired of listening, but I still need to talk." When I say that, it makes them feel like they aren't one of *those* people, and they want to listen.
>
> —Claudia

> I want to tell my friends, "Just say you're thinking of us, that you care, put your hand on our shoulder, don't probe, don't try to make us feel better, don't stay long, maybe drop off a meal and leave. It just helps to know you're thinking of us."
>
> —Courtney

## PARENT SUPPORT GROUPS

A support group can be a valuable source of comfort for parents who have experienced the death of a baby. Other bereaved parents, unlike many friends and relatives, can be sensitive and knowledgeable.

Attending a support group is comforting in many ways. In a positive, accepting group atmosphere, parents can share their grief with others who truly understand. They can talk about their baby and their feelings. Others can validate how significant and painful their loss is, reassure them that their feelings are normal, give them insight on ways to cope, and help them to discover that they are not alone in suffering such a loss or having to have made such difficult decisions.

> It felt like a lifeline, knowing others were surviving this devastating loss. It was a place to talk, and that helped me work through the guilt.
>
> —Jessie

> It helped, just being able to air out some feelings and just the fact that I was doing something positive, was getting out, just somewhere to go every other week, being a part of something. I would have been a lot more desperate if it wasn't for the support group and friends made there, if I couldn't have had anyone to talk to.
>
> —Rose

> The group just made me feel normal in a state where you don't know what to do. I felt like no one could possibly feel this bad, and then I would sit there and hear these people saying the same things that I was thinking myself. It was an incredible comfort.
>
> —Liza

> I just needed a supportive forum in which to voice feelings of anger and isolation, to know the feelings I had were typical. And it's helpful if you go for a period of time to watch people work through their grief and know that there is a point when things begin to improve.
>
> —Holly

Most support groups are free, sponsored by hospitals, hospices, churches or mental health agencies. Most meet for two hours once or twice a month. Parents may attend as many meetings as they wish.

Some groups bring in speakers and then open up for discussion, while others devote the entire time to open discussion. A facilitator may be there to offer information and help guide the discussion, but parents determine the issues by sharing the feelings they are struggling with. If parents do not wish to talk, they should feel welcome just to listen.

Many parents attend support group meetings without their partners. Schedules and babysitting sometimes make it possible for only one parent to attend. Or one partner may not feel a need to attend or may feel reluctant to share private feelings with others. If your partner is reluctant to go with you, you might encourage him or her to attend one or two meetings, just to observe and support you.

Going to your first support group meeting can be scary. You may feel anxious, especially at the thought of sharing your feelings with strangers. It can help to go with someone—your partner, a friend, a relative. Or you can even call the facilitator or another bereaved parent who attends and ask him or her to look for you. These people know how difficult that first meeting can be.

> I wanted to talk to people who had lost a child because I thought that would be helpful. My husband also believes only they would know exactly what it was like. I did seek out people like that. But I never attended a support group. Looking back, I would've benefited from that, but we just couldn't quite get it together. We just missed a lot of connections, and I didn't have the energy to pursue it. I think if somebody pursued it with me, I probably would've gone. Maybe even if somebody had sent me a letter that said, "This is the next meeting exactly and why don't you come?" I needed a push.
>
> —Hannah

Because grieving the death of a baby is so different, parents who experience miscarriage, stillbirth or infant death find that pregnancy/infant loss support groups are far more helpful than general bereaved parent groups.

> After Kevin died, we went to a bereaved parent support group several times, but their children were so much older, even in their 20s, and they had so many memories

and so many other people knew their child and grieved with them. It was hard because Kevin never had a chance to form other relationships besides with me and his dad. He didn't have any friends who also knew him and grieved too. That made us feel worse.

—Cathryn

Some parents do not feel the need to attend a support group. They may feel they are getting enough support from other sources, or the idea of a group just doesn't appeal to them. Other parents may go once and get turned off by the experience. If you go only once, however, you may not be giving it a fair chance. Most groups have open attendance, so the composition can vary from meeting to meeting. Talking and listening to other parents may be more helpful after your shock and numbness have worn off. If you still feel reluctant or skeptical, you may want to go a couple of times or talk with the facilitator about your doubts.

We went once, two weeks after Jessica died, and I didn't like it. They had all lost their babies less recently than me. Then, at two months, my husband started school and I had no support. So I went to the group by myself and met another woman who was struggling with spiritual stuff too, so I called her. She's been my biggest support ever since.

—Rose

Even if you do not like the idea of a group, it can be a good place to meet another parent to connect with. You can continue this relationship outside the group, offering each other the reassurance and understanding that are so helpful. Many parents who lack the support of other bereaved parents feel an extra sense of loneliness and uncertainty about their grief.

It would've helped just to know that I wasn't the only person it happened to. That it wasn't this big mystery and we weren't bad people and that kind of thing.

—Hannah

To see what other people were going through would've given me permission to express my feelings. At the time I was just completely ignorant of what other parents experienced. There wasn't any information out, there wasn't anything that said, "This is a significant loss, this is real and these feelings you're having are normal." I was just real hungry for information and I didn't know that much about what to expect.

—Anya

To find a support group in your area, ask your doctor or contact the social worker at a local hospital, hospice or mental health agency. Newspapers sometimes publish a listing of area support groups. Or you can call or write to one of the national organizations listed at the back of this book.

# COUNSELING

Many parents benefit from individual counseling as well as a support group. Each has its own unique benefits. Attending a support group can help you feel less isolated, offer opportunities to strike up supportive friendships and let you have hope for the future by observing how others have coped. Individual counseling can give you a chance to air your feelings at greater length and help you work through other personal issues. Many parents have particular difficulty dealing with anger or feel overwhelmed by guilt, depression or anxiety. Family therapy can also benefit surviving children and your relationship with your partner.

You could benefit from counseling if any of the following apply:

- you think it might help,
- you feel stuck or worry that you are resisting grief or consumed by it,
- you feel you are falling apart or no longer in control,
- you notice that you are engaging in addictive or destructive behaviors (see chapter 2, "Numbness and Shock" for more signs of repressed grief),
- you continue to find no joy in other aspects of your life and resent others who do,

- your feelings, behavior or physical symptoms interfere with your well-being or your functioning (for instance, your depression prevents you from eating or sleeping, your lack of concentration produces costly mistakes, your headaches or fatigue keep you from enjoying favorite activities),
- you feel isolated or want the comfort of someone who can listen and support you, or
- others—friends, relatives, doctor, clergyperson—tell you they think you might benefit from counseling.

Some people hesitate to enter counseling for fear they will never stop needing it. For many people, getting into therapy implies weakness, mental illness or character flaws. Actually, it indicates personal strength, health and courage because being successful in therapy means facing your feelings, your problems and the truth about yourself. Therapy can help you to

- feel and express a wide range of emotions
- obtain insight into your reactions
- learn new ways of coping
- acquire more skills for working through problems

Eventually, through therapy, you gain the ability to help yourself. When you stop going regularly, your counselor can remain available for occasional consultation.

If nothing else, therapy gives you a chance to talk about your baby. A sensitive counselor can help you express and cope with your feelings. With that special support you will find it easier to come to terms with your baby's death.

Therapy was essential for me, just to be able to go in once a week for an hour and talk about Kevin and go over and over the same stuff. You don't feel like you're imposing because you're paying them to listen; that's *your* time to do whatever you need.

—Cathryn

Counseling really helped me a lot. It was a place where I could go and unload my feelings and learn to cope with them instead of shoving them inside.

—Clara

If you decide to try counseling, look for a licensed professional who has experience working with bereaved persons. A reputable counselor can be a psychologist, clinical social worker, psychiatrist, psychiatric nurse or clergyperson. To locate specialists in your area, contact professional organizations (see appendix B, "Resources for Bereaved Parents") or check the Yellow Pages listings under "Counselors" or "Mental Health Services." Recommendations from people you know can be most valuable. You might ask:

- other bereaved parents
- your doctor
- parent support group facilitators
- the social worker or psychologist at a local hospital
- the women's center or parent education department at a local hospital
- your community mental health clinic
- your church or synagogue
- a hospice organization
- the local college, university or medical school counseling center
- a family service agency

If cost is a concern, community, university and medical school mental health clinics operate on sliding fee scales, so you pay what you can afford. Many private counselors will negotiate their fees. Most health insurance or employee assistance programs will pay some or all of the cost. It may help to remember that *you are worth it.*

## HEALTHCARE PROVIDERS

Parents are profoundly affected by the treatment they receive from healthcare providers. When treated with warmth and empathy, they can be comforted by the fact that someone really cares. Parents are deeply touched by healthcare providers who can share a tear with them and really validate their grief. Any emotional support where feelings are validated can help with coping.

> The pastor, social worker, doctors and nurses kept coming in to check, and I think it was helpful because it made me think, "Well, when you have a baby that's alive, they come in to see how you're doing and how the baby's doing, but if you have a dead one, they don't just leave you out. They treat you like you're human too."
>
> —Martina

> The nurse cried right along with me. You know, there's really something to someone giving validity to your feelings when everybody else is trying to make you feel better. Here this wonderful woman was crying and letting me know I had good reason to cry. She didn't try to shut me up. She wasn't in a hurry. She acted like a regular person who was really feeling sad that this had happened to me and she wasn't scared of what I was going to do next. I could be hysterical and it was OK.
>
> —Sarah

> Our doctor was there for us in a lot of ways. He was unusually sensitive. When we went into his office just a few days after Meghan died, he said, "I want to talk to you about the emotional side of this," and he made a real point to discuss what we could expect to feel. And he was real open about his own feelings. I remember him crying the night we delivered the baby and saying how hard that was for him, that the reason he went into obstetrics was so he could bring life and not have to deal with death so much.
>
> —Jessie

There are no words that can erase your pain. But you can be deeply comforted by the special attention you receive: your doctor's availability to just listen and be with you, your nurse's gentle touch or any special arrangements made for you. Caregivers may also help by handling some of the paperwork, gathering information on funeral homes or sensitizing others to your special situation. Even little gestures that save miniscule moments of pain can make a big difference.

> They did things to make me get well, but also be separate
> from the maternity ward. Since they didn't have facilities
> on that floor, they brought me a portable sitz bath. That
> they cared was real important. You need to feel that you
> are important and not just another one of the patients.
>
> —Bryn

> The hospital social worker was so nice, she wanted to
> listen and she helped us. We didn't know where to start,
> how to bury him or what. We had never had to deal with
> this, and she helped us through the whole thing. She
> called around and she got prices of things. You know,
> that's something to think about. She made you realize
> that you did have to think of cost and not to feel guilty.
>
> —Kelly

> Our pediatrician did stuff that was very helpful in terms
> of making sure we didn't get lost in the system. He told
> the clerks that this family would be coming to see him,
> and it wasn't for a pediatric appointment. So we didn't
> get to the desk and have someone say, "Oh, what are you
> doing here?"
>
> —Hannah

Honesty from your caregivers is as important as warmth, empathy and sensitivity. You needed to know what was happening and to be told the truth about your baby's prognosis. If the doctor was perplexed, you wanted uncertainty rather than phony answers or assurances. To be prepared for the worst is far preferable to being caught unprepared.

> My doctor was very good during the labor, as well as
> right after delivery, about keeping me informed of exactly
> what was happening and what the risks were and what
> the choices were and what things he suggested. Later he

spent a lot of time talking out some of the more philo-
sophical and emotional issues about a kid hooked up to
machines. He was very open, direct and supportive.

—Sophie

My OB was open and sincere. He was sad too, and that
was very helpful. When he came in the second night—he
had just gotten back from seeing the baby at the hospital—he came in and flopped down on a chair and just
buried his head in his hands, and he said, "You know, I
don't know what to tell you." I appreciated that he didn't
come in with some big long dissertation on something. He
just didn't know what to say, and that honesty was so
nice. He acted very sad, and I wanted everybody to be
very sad.

—Sarah

I feel like no one was really geared towards dealing with a
death. None of them would admit for a moment. I kept
trying to find out how bad it was and my pediatrician talked
to me at the hospital and she kept saying, "Things look
bad," but she was the only person that would say it like that
and try to help me get prepared for the worst. I think
everybody else was denying it more than I was. I'm very
angry that the other doctors were not honest with me.

—Liza

## IF HEALTHCARE PROVIDERS TURN AWAY

Parents are very impressionable after a baby dies. If your doctors and
nurses treated you as if your baby's death was insignificant, you may
come away wondering if they are right. If you were treated with
aloofness or evasiveness, you may feel that you are not entitled to
information. You may wonder if you did something wrong to make
your doctors or nurses abrasive, too busy to listen or too uncomfortable
to share your grief.

My doctor was saying things like "products of conception" and "Be grateful that it happened early. You were
hardly pregnant!" I couldn't believe what I was hearing.

Hardly pregnant? My baby was dead and he was telling
me this!

—Mariko

Since I was in labor at twenty-four weeks, we signed a
paper saying we did not want the baby to be resuscitated
if she was born lifeless. Then this doctor said, "I understand you don't want your baby resuscitated," like he was
accusing me of not wanting my baby to live.

—Elaine

I saw my doctor just standing up against the wall, so I've
always felt like there was some grief there, but she just
couldn't share it with me. I've always felt like if she
could've shared that, it would have been a little bit easier
for me.

—Liza

You may have resented your doctor's cool, clinical attitude.
Charlie remembers, "It was *my* wife and *my* baby Kimberlie, and the
doctors were looking at it as another fascinating case." Jessie recalls,
"The doctor kept calling it 'fetal demise.' I felt like he had difficulty
saying 'dead baby.' That really bothered me." Rayleen feels this
clinical attitude undermined her dignity: "They come in and just do
to you whatever they want and after a while your body is just theirs."

If you needed to recuperate in the hospital, you may not have
been given a choice about staying on the maternity ward. You may
have wanted to be with the other mothers and babies because you felt
that's where you rightfully belonged. Or you may have preferred to
be in another ward because you could not bear seeing a mother
cuddling her infant. Unfortunately, some staff on other wards do not
know how to give sensitive care to bereaved mothers, and you may
have felt isolated and forgotten. As Erin recalls, "Nobody knew what
to do with me, so they just avoided me. I felt like a freak, that I did
something wrong." Hannah remembers being disappointed that no
one inquired about her baby's death. She says, "Not one nurse said
anything to me about the baby. It was incredible. I thought somebody
might say *something*!"

*EDUCATING YOUR DOCTOR ABOUT GRIEF*

Unfortunately, some doctors don't know how to support grieving parents. Grief education is not routinely included in medical training, and death is not a regular feature of obstetric or pediatric practice. Just as parents may feel like failures after their baby dies, doctors may also feel helpless. This mutual sense of failure can make parents and their doctor feel awkward with each other.

You may have to enlighten your doctor about the kind of support you need. Just as friends and family may take their cues from you, so may your doctor. Your doctor cannot read your mind, but if you can explain your feelings and concerns, he or she may be responsive to your needs. If you feel like crying, cry. If you have questions, ask them. If you are angry with your doctor, talk to him or her about your feelings. Your doctor can learn from you about the needs of grieving parents, knowledge that may enable him or her to be helpful to you as well as to others. (See appendix A, "A Note to Caregivers.")

If your doctor is unresponsive to your suggestions or if you do not feel comfortable with your doctor, consider finding another one. Other bereaved parents can offer suggestions as to which doctors handle grief and death sensitively. You can ask for consultation appointments with several doctors and explain your situation and needs. Especially if you plan to have another child, you will want a doctor who is sensitive to your needs for reassurance and vigilant medical care without being patronizing. Changing doctors can feel like another loss, but you deserve a doctor who is supportive.

Family doctors, unlike obstetricians and pediatricians, take care of people of all ages—from infants to pregnant women to the elderly. As a result, they are trained to handle death and dying. Since they provide continuity of care during pregnancy, delivery and afterward, they may be quite helpful during your grieving process.

# SPIRITUALITY AND RELIGION

Your spiritual and religious beliefs may help you cope with your grief, or they may make you more confused or angry. Even if you consider yourself devout, it is normal to question your beliefs and even modify them according to the lessons you learn about life and death. Rose notes, "It hasn't lessened my faith in God. I know He's there. But it has changed my perception of what He is and how He reacts to this world." Janet agrees: "I used to see God as all-powerful and rewarding, but now I see Him as no more in control or better than me."

Many mothers struggle with the idea that God took away their baby. It is especially difficult to find comfort in the rationalization "God needed a little angel." As Bess says, "That made no sense to me whatsoever—that now I had my personal angel in heaven, that I should be glad for that. I told the hospital chaplain that I needed David here, and he said God needed him more than I did, and I just disagreed with that!" Courtney concurs, "You'd think after a million years of human evolution He'd have enough little angels." Lena notes, "I was so angry at God that I just told Him to get out of my life. It took a while to get back to the church."

Although you may be struggling with your religious faith, your speculation about what happens after death can be a comfort to you. If you believe that people exist after death, you may hope to see your child again someday. Spiritual philosophies about the purpose of life and death can also help you make sense of it all. Perhaps you believe that what happens in your life is part of a divine or universal plan. Believing that someone or something is in control can help you feel a little less vulnerable.

> I have this in my imagination that Christopher is up there with my grandparents. I have no idea what happens after death, like if we know anybody, but if we do I'm sure my grandparents are having fun with him and I know he's happy. ... I just have to keep remembering that he is in a better place, and that helps a lot. He has the best baby-sitter.
>
> —Rayleen

> I've accepted that what happens is God's will. I felt very strongly that the baby wasn't meant to be. After I'd questioned everything I came to that conclusion and I had to live with that.
>
> —Jane

> Maybe God decided that Nicole was too good to be on the earth and go through the things that we go through. Maybe He needed an extra angel in heaven and He took

her. Maybe He knew that I was going to get divorced and maybe He figured that two kids would be too much for me to handle. I don't know. I just know that He knows what He's doing and maybe He thought through this experience I could help other people.

—Cindy

I feel like God allows everybody a choice of what their life is. You don't know it after you're born, maybe, and it's not predestination, but I feel like we chose and Daniel chose and for some reason we were his parents, and I would rather have had him for three days than none.

—Liza

Part of what I believe is that we exist as a soul or whatever, as an entity, before we are a body. We decide how and when and to whom to be born and what kind of life to lead, which is not to say it's all predestined and cast in stone, because we make changes as we go, but that we have a purpose for being born, almost like something or some things we want to accomplish. And when those get accomplished, then we usually die. Some people accomplish these quickly and some people take a long time, and I had the sense that Stephanie had some particular things that she wanted to do in this lifetime and she had some things to help us learn and she had a reason for being here. ... She needed to know that she was loved, and she knew that the whole time I was pregnant and she knew that the five days she was here and that she wanted to share that love with us, and then she didn't need to stay around any longer. I also had another sense about her—I have a real issue with letting go of all the way from trivial things to people and relationships, and I think one of the things she was here to teach me was how to let go.

—Sophie

Even if you do not consider yourself to be religious, you may discover some spiritual philosophy that gives you answers and helps you cope. (For more ideas, see "Why Me, Why My Baby" in chapter 7.)

# POINTS TO REMEMBER

- Supportive friends and family can help you cope with your baby's death.
- Many people do not know how to be supportive because they are unfamiliar or uncomfortable with death and grief.
- Friends often take their cues from you. Tell your friends what you need. True friends will appreciate your guidance.
- Some friendships will deepen, others will be lost and new ones will form.
- Attending a support group can help you feel less isolated and can reassure you that your feelings are normal and that you will feel better over time.
- Counseling can help you work through difficult feelings and help you cope more easily.
- Healthcare providers can make a tremendous difference in how you cope. Having their support validates the significance of your baby and your grief.
- Religion or spirituality can be a source of comfort. Find some philosophy that helps you cope.

# 10

# Trying Again:
# The Subsequent Pregnancy

When your baby dies, you lose your innocence. Your firsthand experience with tragedy teaches you that there are no guarantees. Whether your baby died early or late in your pregnancy, before or after birth, you may feel anxious about having another baby. There are a number of issues that you will have to face along the way:

- deciding whether to try again
- deciding when to try again
- trying to conceive
- coping during the pregnancy
- preparing for and coping with the birth
- coping after the birth

## SHOULD WE TRY AGAIN?

One reaction to the death of a baby is to insist on never having more children. The risk of going through another pregnancy or becoming attached to another baby may be too much to bear. You may even consider sterilization for you or your partner. Especially if you have had a number of losses, you may simply feel it is time to move in another direction with your life. At the other extreme, if you think another baby would help you cope with your loss, you may want to get pregnant right away to fill the emptiness and ease your sorrow.

Most parents vacillate between the two reactions, month to month, or even minute to minute. One day you claim, "NEVER AGAIN," and the next day you yearn to feel new life inside you. Or you may be certain you want another baby, but you need to gather your courage before trying again. If you have to deal with the possible recurrence of a genetic defect, you may want more information before making a decision about future pregnancies.

> We went back and forth about having another child. Cal wanted to get pregnant right away, and I said, "No, I'm not ready." And then by the time I was ready, we had reversed positions. He was saying, "Maybe we should wait six months or a year." So there was a lot of stress there.
>
> —Sophie

> Since Johanna's heart defect was genetic, the doctor thinks there is a 15 percent chance it will happen again, so we feel anxious about another pregnancy. We'll wait until we can focus on the 85 percent chance that it *won't* happen again.
>
> —Courtney

## WHEN SHOULD WE TRY AGAIN?

Many parents can't even consider trying again in the months following their baby's death. It feels too risky to set themselves up for possible disappointment. Even parents who feel desperate to try again notice that this urge fades over the first few months as their grief intensifies. If you are sure you want to try again, you might consider waiting a few months to see how you feel.

### *YOUR DOCTOR'S ADVICE*
If your baby died during or shortly after your pregnancy, there are certain physical considerations that bear on the timing of another pregnancy. After an uncomplicated pregnancy and vaginal delivery, your doctor may advise waiting three to six months, enough time for the uterus to get back into shape so that it can sustain a healthy pregnancy. If you had a cesarean delivery or complications during your pregnancy, your body may need more time to mend. Ask your doctor about your special needs for physical healing.

Aside from the physical healing, there is emotional healing. Many doctors and psychologists have speculated that after the death of a baby, parents may encounter difficulties relating to the subsequent child. The mother may hesitate to bond during pregnancy, she may be overprotective or she may treat the new baby as a replacement for the dead one. Because of these concerns, many doctors suggest a waiting period of six months to a year, so that the mother can resolve her grief before having another baby.

However, this view is changing as more evidence shows that many mothers do not feel resolved for four or more years. In addition, after a baby dies, it seems only natural that the mother may feel anxious about another pregnancy and overprotective of her children. Finally, many parenting difficulties can be overcome with emotional support, assistance and information on effective parenting. Resolution of grief is not the only key to successful parenting.

Still, many doctors advise their patients to wait six to twelve months. Whatever the time period your doctor suggests, it may seem like an eternity. Jessie points out, "I didn't want to wait a year to start thinking about another baby. I had all this parenting energy and nowhere to direct it." On the other hand, if your doctor tells you to get pregnant right away, you may later resent it because, as Holly says, "It sounded as if, 'Let's just write this one off and move on.' I think it adds to the demeaning of the life that was."

### DECIDING FOR YOURSELF
Most mothers agree that open-ended advice and information are more helpful than a prescribed number of months. With information, you can decide what is best for you as an individual. Deciding for yourself can also restore a sense of control that may have been shattered by your baby's death.

> My doctor said to wait until I felt ready. He said, "They can tell you six months or a year, whatever, but you've got to tell yourself when you're ready because some people can't handle it right away and some people have to get pregnant because they can't handle not having that baby." I was glad he said that because I feel that every person is different. Some people need that baby right then and they want to go right back into a pregnancy—I did at first. ... And if they give you six months or a year, whatever, you figure like that's a time line. If you don't

get pregnant after six months or after a year, whatever, something else is wrong. If they leave it up to you, it makes you feel like you *can* do something right.

—Martina

Waiting six months was something I decided for myself, and that made me feel good because that was one little place I could have control. It really seems like it should be an individual decision, because you know what is best.

—Liza

Deciding for yourself lets you take into consideration your own unique needs and feelings. You may want to contemplate the following questions before making decisions.

- Do you want to have all your children before you are 30, 35, 40 years old?
- Do you want your baby to be close in age to your other children?
- Are you worried that it may take a while to conceive, so you should get started soon?
- Do you feel that having another baby as soon as possible may help you cope with your grief and your emptiness?
- Do you need more time to heal physically?
- Do you need more time to research the cause of your baby's death?
- Do you need to find a supportive doctor or a specialist who can help you get answers?
- Do you feel that waiting a while may help you feel less anxious about the next pregnancy?
- Do you feel that waiting may help you to enjoy the new baby more, so you aren't grieving for one baby and preparing for another at the same time?
- Are you anticipating any big changes in your life— school, job, moving, relationships, other deaths and births in your family?
- How does your partner feel?

## GETTING PREGNANT SOON

Some mothers who get pregnant within six months of their baby's death are simply driven to have a baby. For them, the pregnancy can be a very anxious, grieving time, but a healing thing to do.

> I really felt that getting pregnant soon was what I needed. I was aware of what the problems could be, and it's just hard not to. It's not like you totally have control over it. You try to comply with what you know is best—just from a physical point of view, the chances of having a healthy baby are better if you give your body a certain period of time to recuperate. So I waited as long as I could [four months].
>
> —Hannah

For some mothers, the need to become pregnant is overwhelming. They find that being pregnant fairly soon helps them deal with their loss and erases the feeling of failure. Some mothers report a need to "prove I could do it." The advantages of getting pregnant soon include:

- having the feeling that you're moving on toward more hopeful, joyful times
- overcoming feelings of failure, wanting to be able to "do it right"
- overcoming feelings of anxiety about possible infertility
- overcoming some feelings of emptiness (while the new baby can't replace the baby who died, you want a baby in your arms)
- beating the biological clock
- having the new baby close in age to your older child

Many mothers recognize the emotional and physical disadvantages of getting pregnant so soon, but for some the advantages still outweigh the drawbacks. You may decide that you can't feel any worse at this point, so you may as well risk another loss now, rather than later. You may also find it difficult to use contraception because it feels so counterproductive. (See chapter 3, "Sex and Contraception.")

If you decide to get pregnant before three or six months have passed, there may be people who disapprove. Your doctor and your friends may express concern about your physical or emotional recovery or how you would cope with another loss. But remember, it's not their decision to make. It's your recovery, your body, your pregnancy, your children, your life. It's also your decision.

> It was OK except for the fear. It would've been a calmer pregnancy if I had waited at least a year. But then the aching for a baby overtook the fear. I wanted a baby, so forget the fear, we're having a baby.
>
> —Cindy

> I risked it, losing another baby at a time when I was already vulnerable. I thought I could handle it better than if I got over the grieving process, felt happy about my life, got pregnant, lost another baby. That terrified me more. I couldn't face that, whereas, I thought, "Okay, I'm at the bottom right now and I think I could handle this." I don't understand this advice about waiting a year. For me I think that would've been much worse.
>
> —Bryn

## WAITING TO GET PREGNANT
The advantages to waiting before another pregnancy include:

- having more time to heal physically
- having more time to heal emotionally
- having time between the babies to help you appreciate their individuality and keep them more separate in your mind
- being less anxious during the pregnancy
- being able to enjoy the new baby more because you are grieving less

You may have your own special reasons for waiting a while. If you've had a string of losses, you may need a break, emotionally and physically. If you had physical complications during pregnancy, your body may need extra time to heal, increasing your chances for a healthy baby. There may be other changes in your life, and you want to feel more settled before you try again. Perhaps you have a surviving twin to care for. Perhaps you are a single mother without a steady partner.

Some mothers who try to get pregnant fairly soon end up waiting because infertility or miscarriage postpones a successful pregnancy. Many mothers concede that their bodies and minds may have needed more time to prepare for another pregnancy and another baby. Jessie and Holly finally had success after working through anger and periods of depression. Claudia notes, "When I accepted that my life is full even if I never have a child, then boom—I got pregnant." Hannah agrees: "I think your mind and body know to some extent when you're ready." Bess eventually had a baby a year and a half later, but feels "glad that it happened that way. By then I felt more positive about the future and carrying a new baby. She fit right in, and I could be happy about her."

Some mothers who get pregnant within six months wish they had waited a little while longer. They discover that grieving intensely, being pregnant and then having a new baby is a confusing, unpleasant combination. Typical of these mothers, Sarah admits, "It was just too close. It was all so blended—exhaustion, grief, hormones, being pregnant again, postpartum blues, everything. That first year was a nightmare, even after Gary was born, not knowing what was the cause for my tears that day. I was a mess."

But waiting can be very difficult. You may feel frustrated, in limbo, unable to move toward your goal of having a baby in your arms. Instead of waiting a prescribed number of months, you may want to take your own special needs and situation into account:

- Educate yourself about the advantages and disadvantages of postponing pregnancy. Ask your doctor and other bereaved mothers; find articles and books to read.
- Consider your physical and emotional needs.
- Take it a month at a time. Avoid any pressure to either wait or get pregnant by a specific date.
- Allow yourself a sense of control over your own life.

Remember even if you wait more than six months or a year, getting pregnant can still have a healing impact.

# CAN WE GET PREGNANT?

Once you decide to start trying again, you may feel hopeful because you are doing something positive and moving forward. You may feel as though you are regaining some purpose in your life. You may feel closer to your partner.

Trying again can also be a frustrating, infuriating and nerve-wracking time. You may feel obsessed with trying to get pregnant, as you believe that a baby will fill some of the emptiness you feel. You may feel anxious because you know that this baby will not be the baby you lost. You may feel angry that you have to do this again. As Jessie recalls, "I felt like I'd put in my time being pregnant and I just wanted the baby." You may worry that if you get pregnant, you'll wish you had waited a little longer out of loyalty to your baby or out of fear that you're not ready to love another baby as much.

If you are struggling with infertility, your grief and anxiety can be intensified by the invasive procedures, mechanical timing of sex, and disappointment month after month. Even if you are normally fertile, you may worry if you don't get pregnant after a couple of months.

> The monthly thing of finding out you're not pregnant is a grief every month. After Heidi died, the first miscarriage set me back. Then the second miscarriage and D & C— that was like the final blow. That whole invasion of my body ... that was probably the height of my depression, because I was still grieving over Heidi and frustrated about getting pregnant.
>
> —Holly

Trying again can be especially difficult for parents who have lost one or both twins (or triplets, etc.). There is something special about raising two or more children who were conceived and born together. The parents may feel as though they have lost their only chance, as the likelihood of conceiving another multiple pregnancy is slim. When a subsequent pregnancy is not a multiple one, they may feel added disappointment.

> Losing twins really bothered me more than any other loss. It bothers me just to read about twins or see them. It

hurts to think about twins. I had them fixed in my mind
as something special. It's something I really wanted. A lot
of people think that would be too much work to have
two, but I think it would be fun. I always thought it
would be fun.

—Peg

# THE PREGNANCY

## *VULNERABILITY AND CONTROL*

Some days I thought, "I'm pregnant; the world is great!"
Then other days I'd think, "I've already lost a baby. What
if it happens again?"

—Cindy

Having a baby die, especially during pregnancy or shortly after birth,
will probably color your experience with subsequent pregnancies,
making you more anxious that something could go wrong. You don't
just have abstract knowledge that babies can die. You can't hide
under the assumption that it won't happen to you. It *has* happened
to you, and while the chance of it happening again may be remote, it
is a possibility.

You may feel angry or disappointed that you can't have that
innocence back and enjoy a blissful pregnancy. You may wish that
you could relax, but you can't totally ignore what happened before.
You may feel you simply cannot expect a pregnancy to result in a baby
that will survive. Holly recalls, "All through my pregnancy I thought,
'Yes, I am pregnant, but I don't feel like I'm going to bring anything
home from the hospital.' "

Feeling vulnerable is difficult to cope with. You may feel uneasy
because you know that even if you take good care of yourself and your
baby, your baby can still die. On the other hand, knowing your baby's
cause of death can help you feel some control, that perhaps certain things
can be done to prevent the same thing from happening again.

No matter how well you take care of yourself during a
pregnancy, nothing is guaranteed. I decided that even if
you go into labor it's not guaranteed that you're going to

have a baby. It's not guaranteed when that baby is born
you're going to have a baby. You've just gotta go one day
at a time. After you lose one, it's so hard.

—Martina

The doctors had described a place on my uterus where,
from my miscarriage probably, my uterus wasn't completely healed, so as the next baby was growing, the
placenta was breaking away from the uterus and that's
what was causing the bleeding. It was an abruption.
Knowing the reason helped encourage me that there
wasn't something dramatically wrong with me, that all I
needed to do was wait until I was better healed. It made
me feel like it was a problem that could be solved by time.

—Elaine

Although you can remind yourself that the vast majority of babies
are normal and healthy, the statistical probabilities may offer little
comfort. After all, you "beat the odds" when your baby died. While
intellectually you know everything is likely to turn out fine, it can be
difficult to convince yourself *emotionally*. While you may be certain that
others will have healthy babies, you may feel sure that you won't.

If your anxieties seem overwhelming, the following ideas may
help calm you.

- Remember that having fears about the baby's health and
  development is a common experience among pregnant
  women, even those who haven't faced tragedy.
- Remind yourself that your anxieties and thoughts do not
  have the power to harm your baby or make your fears
  come true.
- Try relaxation techniques (see "Relaxation" in chapter 3).
- Write about your feelings and worries.
- Talk about your fears to someone who can listen and
  offer reassurance that your anxieties are normal but
  most probably unfounded.
- Reduce your stress in other ways. For instance, give up
  unessential responsibilities and set aside time for relaxation.

- Instead of trying to repress your fears, redirect them toward positive imagery. For instance, Courtney acknowledged her fear of heart defects and was able to counteract them somewhat by imagining her baby's heart forming properly during the first critical months of development.

Your anxieties can also be diminished by trying to gain some feelings of control. You may want a lot of information and monitoring during this pregnancy. You can request more ultrasounds and prenatal tests such as amniocentesis. You may make frequent visits to your doctor and listen to the heartbeat every time. You may eagerly wait for the baby to start moving; you may even figure out ways to encourage movement because it can be very reassuring. You may have a lot of superstitions. Or you may find that by giving up some control, you can relax a little because it's out of your hands.

> I remember getting scared, thinking she hasn't moved,
> and I was counting time on the clock. I would count the
> hours. I'd lay down real still and see if the baby would
> kick. I remember holding my belly, holding my baby
> there, and I would talk to her and I just was very hopeful
> that things would be OK with her.
>
> —Bryn

> I had a lot of superstitions. Whatever I did the last
> pregnancy, I didn't do this time. If I went swimming last
> time, I didn't go swimming this time. Things like that.
>
> —Holly

> With the other pregnancies, there wasn't anything I could
> do about it and I just knew it wasn't going to work. This
> time I was more accepting, saying, "Since there isn't
> anything I can do to make it one way or the other, I might
> as well realize that there could be a good outcome, not
> just a bad outcome."
>
> —Meryl

### GETTING PAST A CERTAIN POINT

For some mothers, anxiety is tempered by hope. Especially if this pregnancy is uneventful, you may be able to feel some guarded optimism. As your due date approaches, you may dare to feel that maybe this pregnancy will turn out all right.

> Part of me was *so glad* I was pregnant and part of me was so terrified. I thought, "I can't do this again. I was a fool! Why did I think I could go through this again?" I kept trying to be positive. I did have a feeling she was going to be OK.
>
> —Bryn

Depending on when your baby died, you may feel that if you make it past that certain point, you can relax a little. If you didn't make it beyond the first trimester, you may hold your breath until you get well into the second trimester. If your baby died during the third trimester, your anxiety may intensify then.

> From my twenty-second to my thirtieth week I was nervous about everything, and time just went so slowly. I can remember thinking, "I have to get through one more week and one more week and one more week. ..." You're waiting and hoping nothing happens, and that was probably the worst time. Once I reached thirty weeks, then I think I relaxed quite a bit.
>
> —Peg

Some mothers find it hard to relax at any point. If you make it past the first trimester, you may worry about making it to full term. Even if the baby is born healthy, you may worry about your baby surviving the first six months or the first year. And even if your child survives infancy, another pregnancy, another baby can rake up all those anxieties again.

You may feel very impatient for your due date to arrive so that you can have your baby safely in your arms. Or you may wish that you could just remain pregnant, that your baby is safer inside you.

> The first three months, everything's OK if you don't lose the baby, and then usually the middle months are OK,

and then pray from six to nine that you don't go into
premature labor, and then pray that you don't have a
stillborn.

—Cindy

The whole nine months, I swore it took nine years. It was
the longest nine months I've ever been through. But I
didn't want it to be time to have her because I just kept
having these pessimistic feelings, so why hurry it.

—Martina

## BONDING TO YOUR BABY DURING PREGNANCY

After the trauma of losing a baby, most mothers hesitate to bond with
the subsequent baby. Your joy and expectations are clouded by fears
and pessimism. You can feel totally committed to this pregnancy and
you desperately want to count on having a healthy baby, but at the
same time you worry about the devastation you would feel if this
baby died. Many mothers remain reserved because they dare not pin
their hopes on a positive outcome.

While he was still in the womb, I consciously would sit
and pat and rub and talk, which I didn't do much with
the others, but I kind of thought I'd give him a little extra
advantage. It made me feel good, but I also knew that
now I was feeling attached and that was hard—on the one
hand being told, "Don't get your hopes up too high," but
thinking, "There's no way that I can't feel something!"

—Meryl

For many mothers, preparing the nursery and collecting baby
things, thinking about names, even feeling the baby move, seems too
hopeful. You may wallpaper the baby's room in a pattern that would
also be appropriate for a guest room or a den. When you first perceive
fetal movement, you may be hit with the stark reality of your baby's
presence and how awful it would be if this baby were to die too. You
may wait until your last month to think about names. You may wait
until the baby comes home before you prepare the nursery.

Sarah remembers how doubtful and cautious she was: "I wanted
to pretend I wasn't pregnant. I packed up the nursery. I wasn't into

maternity clothes or little pregnancy conversations, none of that. I was going to wait and *see* if I got a baby!" Hannah postponed baby showers and shopping until *after* Michael came home. Lena concurs, "I didn't want to go buy a bunch of stuff and have this one die too." Even after Bryn's daughter was born, she recalls, "I was afraid to buy diapers above the newborn size because, 'What if she didn't make it?' I was still just taking it a day at a time." For many mothers, superstitions add to their caution. Kitty notes, "I've always been superstitious, even with my first. I didn't want to start the nursery too early in case something would happen."

If you have kept the nursery set up, you may be very protective of its contents. Cindy remembers not letting anyone borrow her baby things until she had a baby of her own to use them. If you put the nursery away, you may hesitate getting things out again because preparing for a new baby triggers memories about the baby who died. This may be difficult, but you can grieve for your missing baby while you look forward to another one. Dara recalls, "Bringing out all her baby things brought everything back into focus again, but it didn't feel *worse*."

Not wanting to feel too attached to your new baby is a common experience. As your pregnancy progresses, your confidence may grow and you may allow yourself to feel a greater bond with this baby. Especially in the months after the birth, you will acquire the full depth and joy of maternal love.

## LOOKING FORWARD, LOOKING BACK

Many mothers find it difficult to be pregnant and to prepare for another baby while grieving for the baby who died. Some parents who avoid grief believe that it is best to move on to the future without looking back. However, avoiding grief thwarts emotional needs and can make parents less capable of emotionally nurturing their new baby. Others believe that the subsequent baby can somehow replace the one who died or erase the need to grieve. But, as Clara realizes, "Being pregnant is great, but it doesn't fix everything; it doesn't banish my grief."

Although it is challenging, it is possible to manage these competing feelings—to express hope for the future *and* grief for the past. Continuing to work through grief enhances your adjustment to your baby's death and prepares a healthy foundation for your relationship with the subsequent baby. (See chapter 7, "How Do I Resolve My Grief?")

During pregnancy, you may imagine the new baby will be similar to the baby who died, as the hope that this baby survives merges with the wish that the other baby had lived. You may even feel that the baby who didn't survive is reborn in some way with the new baby.

> When I was pregnant, I did think about Christopher. I never thought it was the same pregnancy, but it was hard to believe it was another person, another child. It was really hard for me to imagine there could be two of them. I *knew* it was another, but I know I thought about him.
>
> —Rayleen

Intellectually, you know it is not the same baby, but especially before the birth, it is easy to believe that your subsequent baby holds the essence of your other baby. As long as you can appreciate the unique biological and spiritual identity of this new child, imagining similarities can be a harmless way to hold on to the baby you miss so much. After this baby is born and you become acquainted, you will find it easier to keep the babies separate. (See chapter 11, "The Replacement Child.")

### WISHING FOR A CERTAIN SEX

Most parents have a strong preference for the sex of the new baby. If your only daughter or your only son died, you may hope to have another of the same sex. You may feel disappointed if you don't get your wish. If you do get your wish, you may feel very grateful.

> After Jenni died, when I got pregnant I really, really wanted another little girl. Then I had Dustin, and I love him dearly, but I had my heart set on a girl. I think about trying again, having another baby, but with no guarantees, it doesn't seem like the thing to do.
>
> —Maya

> I had done everything. I had known when I was ovulating, so there was no doubt in my mind it was a girl. Even through the whole pregnancy I was telling people it was a

girl. When Chris was born, I remember feeling disappointed and I felt like a jerk because I thought, "You're disappointed in the sex of your child?" But you wonder, "If I hadn't lost the other baby, I would've had a girl."

—Elaine

We wanted a girl, not just because Melanie was a girl, but because, you know, the perfect family, a boy and a girl. For some reason I didn't think I was going to have a girl, so when I did I was just really happy. It took me a couple days to really realize that I had a normal healthy baby and it was a girl, everything I wanted.

—Kitty

I was happy when I had Max, because I really never thought I'd have a boy. I always thought I was going to just have girls, that I wasn't meant to have a boy.

—Jane

On the other hand, you may hope your subsequent baby is the other sex, in order to keep them separate or avoid feeling as though you've replaced the baby who holds a special place in your heart. Bryn observes, "I think maybe it's good that I had a girl. If I'd had another boy, I wonder if maybe my memories would have meshed into one." Martina agrees: "We didn't want a boy because we were afraid we'd try to put the boy in Greg's place."

I was thrilled she was a little girl. It was nice because I immediately saw that I couldn't go through with my little fantasy, that if it was a little boy, it would be the same little boy. And that would've been pretty strong because at birth she looked so much like him. ... But sometimes I wish I had another little boy so that I'd see a little bit more of what he would be like.

—Liza

## SUPPORT

You need a compassionate doctor who attends to your anxieties. To get the reassurance you need, you may want to ask for more tests and more monitoring than usual. It is normal to want to hear the heartbeat, check your progress and pay more attention to details. If your doctor seems too casual about your concerns, you may feel more worried or angry and less in control. Try to find a doctor who respects your feelings and works with you to have a healthy baby. A concerned doctor should be willing to schedule extra time and additional appointments, thus showing a commitment to you and your baby.

Jessie remembers how attentive and dedicated her doctor was; he even lent her a stethoscope so she could listen to the heartbeat whenever she wanted that reassurance. Rayleen recalls, "When the twenty-seventh week came along, I was just really bothered. My doctor said I could come in every week, every day if I had to. That helped." If complications arise during this pregnancy, you will be especially anxious and want additional care and reassurance. In Peg's case, her doctor's extra attention helped her to comfort herself:

When I was about 30 or 32 weeks pregnant with Justin, I started bleeding and I was a basket case. At that time they had already put a cerclage in [wrapped a string around the cervix to keep it closed] and I was taking terbutaline [medication to stop contractions]. I remember I had a doctor's appointment that day and I was getting ready to go and I started bleeding and I thought, "Okay, take a deep breath, calm down. ... You're farther along than you've ever been before, so even if something happens, you're going to have this baby." And I went to 38 weeks with him.

—Peg

Some mothers stop going to their support group after they get pregnant again. To hear about babies dying may make them more pessimistic or anxious during their pregnancy. Jessie recalls, "That was the only negative part about being in the support group. Now we knew 101 ways that babies can die, even things we never used to worry about." For other mothers, going to a support group or at least staying in touch with those parents gives them an opportunity to talk about their anxieties about the new baby, as well as their continuing sadness about the baby who died.

Some hospitals have organized "subsequent pregnancy" support groups for parents who have already experienced the death of a baby. These groups can help parents cope with their anxiety as well as connect them with others who can accompany them through this experience.

# THE BIRTH

The final weeks of your pregnancy may be an especially anxious time. The "moment of truth" approaches. You may constantly monitor your baby's movements or visit your doctor daily. You may try to keep busy to distract yourself from the worry. Even if you feel too scared to count on bringing home a baby, as the due date draws near you may find yourself hoping and feeling optimistic, even as your anxiety mounts. When you're getting ready for the birth, you may feel an odd mixture of impatience and dread, elation and anxiety, optimism and pessimism.

> During the last weeks I felt increasing terror, especially since it was only a year before that I delivered another baby. It was such a blend: it was hard to figure out the grieving, the hormones are going crazy and just being pregnant you're a mess anyway. I can't even compare pregnancies. You go into one pregnancy excited to see your baby and you go into the next one being sure the baby is going to be dead.
>
> —Sarah

> I felt anxiety and fear, but also a little bit of investment, looking forward to it. I actually went out a few days before she was born and bought a dress for her to wear home from the hospital.
>
> —Holly

> I couldn't wait to have him. I was so anxious for him to be born. I wasn't worried so much about the birth part of it, but just to have him here with everything going right. … I wanted to have this baby. The doctor took my cerclage out when I was thirty-seven weeks and nothing happened. After months of stopping premature labor, we

thought, "When we take this out there's nothing that's going to hold this baby back," but nothing happened. I kept waiting and waiting and waiting and finally, a week later, I went into labor.

—Peg

If you are anxious about your baby during contractions, having a fetal monitor can be reassuring. If you deliver by cesarean, you may want to be awake to feel more in control, or you may wish to have a general anesthetic to spare yourself the anxiety. As Martina recalls, "I didn't want to be awake in case something was wrong." Even if labor and delivery go well and you have a healthy baby in your arms, you still may worry. Bryn remembers, "I was happy, but also afraid and nervous. I got to hold her, but I still couldn't trust that everything was going to be OK."

Many mothers are afraid of losing control during labor or being consumed with grief and thoughts of the baby who died. Similarities between your present and past experiences can haunt you. Bryn recalls, "When she was born, everything I was going back to was my first experience—all the rooms, the doctors, the procedures ... I was terrified when my water broke because that's when it all started before." Sophie remembers, "I was afraid I would get real crazy in terms of thinking about Stephanie and crying and sobbing uncontrollably, and that wouldn't help labor at all." But Sophie, like most, found she was able to focus on the present birth. Focusing on the differences between this experience and the other can help you cope and feel more optimistic.

They had the monitor on me and just knowing that her heartbeat was OK, I felt good about it. But I know I was scared too. It's getting close, but you still don't know what's going to happen.

—Rayleen

The first thing I said was, "Is he breathing?" I wanted to make sure he was alive. I think I was so enthralled that this baby came out alive.

—Erin

When Nicole was stillborn it was so quiet. It seemed like the whole hospital got quiet, and you could hear a pin drop, it was so quiet and peaceful. When Emily was born, it was so loud. Everybody was talking and laughing and crying, and so it was a really big difference. I loved the noise.

—Cindy

Whether you waited two months or two years before getting pregnant, feelings of grief may intensify after your new baby's birth. Even if you feel as though you have put your grief behind you, having this baby in your arms can trigger emotions you've yet to express and work through. You may come to another level of realization that the baby you lost will never be recovered, even by having this baby. As Laura points out, "You always hope deep down that maybe another child could fill the void in your heart."

Some mothers try to suppress their grief so it won't dampen their joy. By stifling emotions you won't feel sad, but you won't feel happy either. Bryn recalls, "I was so happy and yet I could still not enjoy it. I was not ready to really enjoy anything. I couldn't savor things." If you permit yourself to feel sad emotions, you also open yourself up to feel the happy ones. Finding a balance rather than trying to repress feelings will benefit you and your baby.

Once you have a real living baby and you see that you're actually dealing with a baby, then it really made me start to think about the other babies quite a bit. I went through a period where it was bothering me more than it had before. ... My grief was something I felt I had pretty much gotten over, and then when I had Justin it brought it back to me and I realized, "It still bothers me."

—Peg

Within a couple of days I was really starting to grieve again. I think a lot of it was probably relief, and maybe I had suspended some of the grief during the pregnancy. I remember while I was in the hospital, just crying a lot, carrying her around, just being so happy with her. At the same time, it seems like I really got a lot of that grief out the first month.

—Liza

I thought having another baby would make me feel better, and during the pregnancy I had something to look forward to, but after Alysia's birth, something was gnawing at me. I've been feeling angry and feeling strongly that I should have another baby. Then last week it dawned on me that I want another baby because it feels like a baby is missing—Steven is missing. I wish I didn't miss him so much, and I thought I'd feel better and go forward instead of backwards.

—Alison

Instead of trying to leave your baby and your memories behind, you might try to take those memories with you, forward into the future. This can help you feel less discouraged. (See chapter 12, "Remembering Your Baby and Moving On.")

## ANOTHER LOSS

After Laura died, I had a miscarriage and that was real hard. It was depressing. It made me think, "Maybe I really am not going to be a mother." I felt like a victim, like maybe there was something out there that was going to get me, and that was a bad feeling.

—Hannah

The miscarriage hurt too. It was like, add another one to the list. When I think about getting pregnant—I had a miscarriage, I had a stillbirth, I had an almost-premature baby—I mean, what's going to happen next?

—Cindy

To have these miscarriages that once again you had no answers for and you couldn't control ... the miscarriages really compounded my grief and just made it more difficult to keep going, to function, to *want* to continue. I just would have rather been dead. The pain was unbearable sometimes.

—Holly

It kept building for me, because the more times it happened, then I thought the less chance I ever have of having
a baby, that there was nothing that could be done. So I
did get more anxious with each one.

—Peg

After your first loss, your greatest fear is that it will happen again. If
it does, it can be devastating. You may wonder if it's a sign of deeper
problems, a prelude to chronic infertility or an inability to bear a
healthy baby. After a number of losses you may feel more anxious
than ever when you are pregnant. You may fear that you could never
survive another loss. But you are probably more resilient than you
think. And you will probably gather up the courage to try again.

## POINTS TO REMEMBER

- For many parents, the decision to try again is a difficult one.
- Give yourself a few months to think about the timing, even if you know you want to try again.
- In deciding when to get pregnant, there are many physical, emotional and logistical factors to consider.
- There are advantages to waiting and there are advantages to getting pregnant fairly soon. Weigh these advantages according to your unique situation and needs.
- When trying to get pregnant, you may feel anxious, angry, obsessed, ambivalent or mechanical, but many parents also feel more hopeful about the future.
- During your pregnancy, it is normal to feel anxious and hesitant about investing in the baby or a positive outcome.
- It is normal to have strong preferences about your new baby's sex.
- During your pregnancy, it is normal to feel that the new baby and the baby who died are similar or somehow the same.
- It is important to have a supportive doctor who is considerate of your anxieties and needs for attentive care.
- A supportive friend or partner can help by listening to you talk about your hopes and fears for this baby.
- During the birth, it is normal to think about your previous experiences.
- After the birth, it is normal for you to grieve deeply, as having another baby can act as a catalyst for your emotions about the baby who died.
- If you experience the death of another baby, you can use what you have learned about grief and gathering memories. You will survive this one too.

# 11

# Raising Subsequent Children

Most parents find that the death of a baby profoundly affects their relationship with the children born afterward. Parents often mention a heightened appreciation for these precious children, overprotective feelings, wanting to be the best parent possible and comparing babies. These reactions can be, but are not necessarily, unhealthy or detrimental. By educating yourself about the effects other parents have noticed, you can be on the lookout for ways to enhance your relationship with your subsequent children. Moreover, you can be reassured that your feelings are normal.

You may also notice changes in your relationship with your children born before the baby died. While this chapter focuses on subsequent children, you may also apply it to your older children.

## HEIGHTENED APPRECIATION

Many parents feel an enhanced appreciation for their subsequent children. These children may seem very precious because, after experiencing the death of a baby, parents don't take for granted the health and survival of their children. Kara notes, "You realize things aren't forever and you appreciate everything they do and what they are." You may feel closer to your children. You may really enjoy them and consider them special. Jane elaborates: "I view Jenny as a child that wouldn't have been if I hadn't lost the other one." Like most parents, you may consider this appreciation to be one of the positive lessons learned from the death of your baby.

You may feel vulnerable when you think how special your children are because it seems you have that much more to lose should tragedy strike. You may feel especially invested if you decide to have only one child after your baby dies.

# OVERPROTECTIVENESS

When he was jaundiced at birth I was sure that he had liver problems; the first cold, I was sure it was pneumonia. Everything that kid did I was sure was going to end his life. I didn't leave that baby with a sitter for over a year. I did not let that child nap without my interrupting the nap for a year. I was terrified he was going to die and I was gonna be sure that I was going to be there when he did. I didn't even want to leave him with my husband because I just knew that if something happened to him and I wasn't there, that would be it for me, if that happened with two kids. I remember thinking, "I will just definitely kill myself then, definitely."

—Sarah

Overprotective feelings naturally arise from firsthand experience with the death of a baby. It is normal to worry and to feel more vigilant about protecting your children from harm. You may feel that tragedy can strike at any time, without warning. You may feel that life is very tenuous, that you can't count on everything turning out all right. Many parents find that these overprotective feelings linger for years, but they are most apparent through the first year or so after a new baby is born. You may also feel overprotective of your older children, even though you felt relatively carefree before your baby died.

All parents worry about their children, but I think there's a certain amount of denial that exists that allows you to not really believe in your heart that something is going to happen to them. And then when something *does* happen to one of your children, you know it can happen, you know it's for real.

—Anya

I think about the fact that she could die, probably more than most parents, and that scares me. I don't think most parents think about that or want to, but it's reality. It could happen.

—Cindy

After the baby died, I would lay in bed worrying about my 2-year-old. I was afraid that something was going to happen to her, and then my other baby would be gone.

—Jane

I was never afraid when Donna was little. Then, after I lost the baby, I was so overprotective—here she was, 10 years old, and I couldn't let go.

—Martina

In particular you may feel vulnerable to:

- fears that you won't be able to keep this baby
- fears that the baby will have a life-threatening illness or accident
- fears about the baby dying during sleep

Parents vary on how vulnerable they feel, but it is normal to have these fears, as well as others. As time passes and your child survives infancy, it may become easier to relax, but you may always feel susceptible to the fact that this child too could die.

### FEARS THAT YOU CAN'T KEEP THIS BABY

In the months after your new baby's birth, you may feel anxious that this baby isn't yours to keep. You may feel as though the baby belongs to someone else, or you may be convinced that the baby will die or be taken away. Kitty remembers, "I didn't fall instantly in love with her because I felt like someone was going to snatch her away, just like with Melanie." Martina agrees: "Up until she was about a year old, I went through times of feeling like I was taking care of a baby that wasn't mine, that she wasn't really ours and someone was going to come and take her and I wouldn't see her again."

I was prepared for anything, if anything happened. I was amazed that I could have a baby that was healthy. I felt

close to her immediately, but it took me a long time to
really believe that everything was going to be fine. I didn't
want to let her out of my sight. The first year I was totally
frightened all the time that something would happen to
her.

—Liza

These feelings can provoke a lot of anxiety, especially since they
are often accompanied by the feeling that you have little control. Over
time, however, you will feel more confident that this is your child to
keep.

## FEARS OF ILLNESS OR ACCIDENT

Even if your baby is robust and healthy, you may worry about a mild
illness turning into a life-threatening situation. You may be anxious
about rare or undiscovered diseases attacking your infant. You may
be on guard against accidents such as choking, falling or car wrecks.
Rose sums up her fears: "With Lori, I just never knew. I thought if she
didn't have some kind of problem internally, that she would die of
SIDS. If she didn't die of SIDS she'd die of something else, get hit by
a car, whatever." If your child does have health problems, your
overprotective feelings can be intensified. Do be careful that you
don't overcompensate for your protective urges by ignoring signs of
illness or neglecting hazardous situations. This could actually endanger
your child's health and safety.

I always worried about him choking on something and I
always thought I was going to feed him Cream of Wheat
until he was 5 so I would never have to worry about him
choking. I have had a first-aid class so I know what to do,
but that doesn't mean I could do it if I had to. I think of
all these off-the-wall things that could happen to him.

—Peg

I can handle a little sickness, but if they get really sick, I
become very uptight and supersensitive to them. Like the
time Kim had pneumonia when she was 16 months old
and I immediately escalated that into something really
life-threatening. Unfortunately, when Jared was 8 days

old we discovered he had meningitis, which *is* life-threatening. He was admitted to the hospital and was on antibiotics, and we just sort of lived there for a while. It was real scary because I thought, "This baby is going to be taken away from me too."

—Anya

He got a rash and I didn't want to rush him to the doctor. I didn't want to be one of *those* mothers because I had been to the doctor so much, and I thought, "We're not going to start this." Then it turned out to be a serious staph infection!

—Desi

## FEARS ABOUT YOUR BABY'S SLEEP

Many parents feel anxious when the baby is sleeping. A sleeping baby is so still and quiet, you may feel compelled to check the baby's breathing often during naps and at night. You may be afraid to leave your sleeping baby alone, as if by being there you can somehow provide a protective shield to ensure your baby's survival. Watching or checking your baby can help reassure you that your baby is safe and sound.

Lena remembers often waking up in the night and touching her baby's face "to make sure he was still warm." Rose recalls, "I never let her out of my sight. Many times I would lay there and just watch her nap for two hours rather than getting up and doing anything. I thought she was going to die any time I couldn't see her."

Particularly in the first few months, some parents panic when the baby is quietly sleeping. To reassure themselves, they sometimes wake the baby.

I think it's a fear that stays there after you lose a baby. Every five minutes I was over there, "If you're not breathing, kid, or I can't see you move, you're waking up!" It's not as bad now, but I'm constantly watching her to see if she's still breathing.

—Martina

Every night I would put my hand on her back to make
sure I could feel her breathing, and if I couldn't, I'd try
and do something that would make sure she'd breathe.
She started sleeping through the night very early and that
scared me. One time she slept through the night and I was
thinking, "I've got to get some rest, so I want to sleep in,"
but there's another part of me thinking, "What happens if
I get up and find out ... ?" So there would be mornings
when I was afraid. "Is she just sleeping late or is something wrong?" I couldn't enjoy sleeping in.

—Bryn

If you consider yourself to have a lot of control over what
happens or if you hold on to the belief that you can somehow prevent
tragedy from occurring, you may feel especially vigilant. You may
even worry that such close monitoring is compulsive, but if checking
the baby helps you feel less anxious, do it.

## HARNESSING YOUR OVERPROTECTIVENESS

Many parents are concerned about being overprotective. Especially
as your children grow older, you may try to hide it, disguise it or
control it in order to encourage their natural curiosity and exploration.

I do worry that I'm too overprotective of him. I tend to
try and protect him from things. With my first pregnancy
I planned to go right back to work, and now here he is,
he's going to be home for two more years. He went to
preschool for six weeks and he hated it, and so I said "If
the kid hates it, why should he go?" and consequently he
hasn't gone back since. I'm not sure he's going to ever go
to kindergarten. And I think if all this had never happened to me with my first child, I would have said, "Too
bad, you don't like preschool. You go to preschool—kids
your age go to preschool—you go!"

—Sarah

It can be very hard to let go and allow your children to experience
any independence, challenge or difficulty. Leaving your child with a
sitter may be doubly hard at first. You may want to cling to your

children, to give of yourself, so that they will have everything they need from you. There are times when this is appropriate, but part of helping your children grow is letting them experience independence when *they* are ready. By holding on, you give your children the impression that the world is a dangerous place. By letting go, yet remaining available, you give your children the security to become independent, the confidence to meet challenges and the courage to overcome difficulties. It helps to remember that attending to your children's need for dependence *and* independence is part of being a responsive parent.

Remind yourself that

- you can't always have control over things that happen,
- some situations *are* harmless,
- expressing your feelings of anger and hurt over your baby's death may reduce some of the anxiety associated with your overprotective urges, and
- as you learn to let go, you may feel a sense of triumph over your worries.

The loss has made me overprotective of Emily, and they warned me about that, and I am. The other day we went to a park with one of my girlfriends, and she has a girl who's three days older than Emily. Her little girl went over to the slides and just started playing. And I thought, "I can't let Emily go down the slide by herself; I can't sit back and let her do it alone! I have to be there and stand there!" But I can't go in the sand since I have a cast on my foot, so I had to decide—let her go or she won't be able to play. And I let her go and it was really hard. She got up those slides and did like every other kid, and it was a good feeling to me. I said, "Wow, I let her go and she did it!" I didn't even realize I could do that ... and it made me realize I was overprotective. It was hard sitting there watching, believe me, but the next time it won't be so hard. ... I think it'll get easier as I get older, as I grow more and realize that I have to give her that space. As she gets older too, I'll trust her balance more.

—Cindy

Fortunately, many parents notice that as their children grow older and thrive, they can relax a little more. Especially if your baby remains in good health and develops normally, you can be reassured that there are no hidden problems. As time passes, you can feel more confident and less vulnerable; you can build some trust that this baby will survive. Cindy remembers, "In her first bath she screamed and I cried, so my mom bathed her. Now I dunk her in there and say 'You're OK.' I feel more comfortable now since we lived through the newborn period."

Later, if you decide to have another baby, you may be more relaxed even during infancy. Your overprotective feelings will diminish as you become accustomed to having a healthy child, but even so, you may always worry about tragedy because you know it can happen.

> The doctor kept saying, "She's fine. Don't think about the past." I couldn't help it. I couldn't help but say life is very tenuous, you cannot count on it. I kept waiting for her to get older because I'd say, "When she gets to be 6 months old I'm going to feel a lot more at ease." When she was 6 months old, I was saying, "When she's a year old I'm going to feel so much better." I still don't have a guarantee, but I'm not afraid like I was. I was nervous when she was a little baby, but now that she's getting older I feel more free.
>
> —Bryn

> I had a successful baby. Lori was alive and well, and I knew I could do it. A baby of mine could live past five days. So with Anna, I'm probably raising her a little bit more normally. I've gotten in the routine of having healthy kids and I know that they'll probably be fine. I'm over those paranoid feelings, other than little surges of panic. I don't think Anna is going to die every time I leave her in the bedroom.
>
> —Rose

# WANTING TO BE THE BEST PARENT POSSIBLE

Like many parents, you may want to be the best parent possible out of a sense of responsibility to do the right thing with your precious children. You may feel extra devoted and take your parenting very seriously.

Wanting to do your best is a positive goal. Your heightened awareness can enable you to be a more conscious parent. You may carefully evaluate your parenting style and work toward becoming a nurturing and firm but flexible parent. You may decide to work on communication skills instead of yelling at or spanking your children. You may decide to learn how to discipline in ways that teach and encourage your children, rather than using punishment.

> I think you better appreciate something that's harder to get. I think he's more special. I would hope that I would treat any baby that I had well and do my best, but I think it just makes me more aware of how much I did want him and how special babies really are and that you're really responsible once you have them for how they grow up.
>
> —Peg

> I think I'm more patient or more tolerant of some things than I would have been if I hadn't lost a baby. Not to the extent of not feeling comfortable stopping certain things, but it just makes you stop and think, "Is this really important?" You know, he might not even be here. I'm concerned about doing the right thing, the right parenting things. I want to do things that are basically good for him. I want to provide him with good experiences. I don't believe in Super Baby, but I want to give him the best, be a good parent.
>
> —Hannah

> I think just being there for him and loving him and giving him security so he can grow, to me is the most important thing that I can do for him.
>
> —Sarah

## DISCIPLINING YOUR PRECIOUS CHILDREN

In striving to be the best, some parents find it hard to set limits with subsequent children. You may find it difficult to allow your children to feel any frustration or disappointment. You may feel they have a special entitlement to everything they want.

> With Lori I think maybe that I've created a lot of bad habits—the fact she won't take a nap because I never let her. I never got those good disciplines started. Life was totally undisciplined. Whatever occurred to me—if I felt like holding her all day, I'd hold her all day. I was never real disciplined with her, so she's not a real disciplined child.
>
> —Rose

Your children will benefit if you try to set reasonable limits. Some parents hesitate to set limits because they don't want to control their children or enforce rules with punishment. However, setting limits actually refers to *discipline*, which means teaching and encouraging, *not* controlling and punishing. Discipline, which is far more effective than punishment, includes:

- remaining friendly with children, and being firm but flexible
- listening to your children's feelings, needs and ideas
- getting to the root of problems
- negotiating solutions
- letting your children make choices between acceptable alternatives

For example, a child may refuse to wear snow pants. Instead of forcing him to wear them, an effective parent might listen and discover that snow pants make him feel babyish. Then, together, they can negotiate a solution—perhaps long underwear or heavy sweatpants. Or the parent can offer a choice: "If you put them on, you can play in the snow; if not, you can play inside." Parents can give even a toddler choices, such as "Do you want to come upstairs by yourself or do you want me to carry you?" or "Do you want to get dressed now or in five minutes?" or "Which vegetable do you want, carrots or broccoli?" Children also respond to this consequence: "If you make a *good* decision, I won't have to decide for you."

Instead of inviting power struggles, this gentle but firm guidance helps your children learn self-control, responsible behavior and how to make good decisions. For more parenting ideas, PET (Parent Effectiveness Training) and STEP (Systematic Training for Effective Parenting) are both excellent programs. Both classes and books are available in most communities. (See "Books on Parenting" in Bibliography.)

Your children will also benefit if you maintain a balance between your needs and their needs. Your needs for sleep, relaxation and order are just as important as their needs for attention, nurturing and spontaneity. The best way to meet your children's needs is by getting your own needs met too. You can't make a withdrawal if your account is empty!

It is natural to feel exasperated with your children. Peg comments, "I do sometimes lose my patience and I try not to do that. I try to deal with things rationally. ... That's hard sometimes with a 2-year-old." Sarah recalls, "I was holding Gary at like three o'clock in the morning and I was thinking, 'WHY don't you go to sleep?!' and feeling so guilty for even getting the least bit angry at this kid." Parenting can be exhausting and frustrating. Sometimes it is a burden you resent. You are entitled to these feelings.

> Being able to sit down and have a cup of tea ... . With a toddler, they want you up and around. I get selfish and then I feel guilty because I wanted this child so bad and now I'm upset because I can't have thirty minutes to myself. We put him to bed at eight o'clock, but that's still not enough time.
>
> —Desi

> My support group kept telling me not to feel guilty if there are times when I think, "Why did I do this?" You've got to know that there will be times when you say, "Why am I a parent?" You know, you're up at three in the morning, your kid is really sick, you're afraid for them and all this. I think it was good that they told me it's OK to have those normal feelings of "What did I do this for?"

because you think you've got to always be sold on
motherhood because you lost a baby and you don't have
the right to complain about your baby.

—Bryn

It is OK to resent or feel irritated with your children. It doesn't
mean you deserve them any less. When you are feeling stressed, take
some time for yourself, even if you have to hire a sitter, call a friend
or lock yourself in the bathroom. Find constructive ways to express
your feelings instead of taking them out on your children or yourself.

Being the best parent doesn't mean being perfect or selfless. You
may wish everything could be perfect, but this is unrealistic and unfair
pressure to put on yourself. Instead, strive to do your best. Being the
best means appreciating your children for who they are, nurturing
and respecting them *as well as yourself* and learning from your
mistakes.

I had some idea that there was some kind of perfect
parent and I was going to do that, that I would never
scold her, and I just let my imagination go wild with me. I
felt like I could just be Super Mom because of what had
happened. It's been kind of a shock to find out that I'm
pretty ordinary. ... I somehow thought I could read all the
books and be a perfect mother, and it's been difficult to
realize that no one has all the answers and that I really
have to go from day to day.

—Liza

I think I'm doing a good job now. I think some of the things
I've done with Lori now I would do differently. I'm not
continuing bad habits. I'm trying to be a lot more disci-
plined with her and setting limits, boundaries with her.

—Rose

## THE REPLACEMENT CHILD

According to psychological and medical literature, the replacement
child syndrome occurs when parents idealize their dead child and
seek to "replace" that child by having a new baby. When the new

baby is born, the parents may have difficulty focusing on this child as an individual separate from the child who died, even imposing expectations for the new baby to be like the dead child. This new baby then grows up in the shadow of the dead sibling.

Naturally, this syndrome is considered unhealthy, especially for the new baby. Thus, parents who have had a baby die may worry about falling into that trap. However, there are a couple of other replacement feelings that are benign and very common among bereaved parents:

- the feeling that you had another baby because you didn't have the one who died, in effect having another baby to fill your empty arms
- comparing your babies, wondering if your dead baby might have been similar to the new baby

Many parents worry about seeing the new baby as a replacement. However, at some point you will realize that no other baby can replace the baby who died. Although this realization can be painful, it is an important step toward recognizing that your subsequent child is an individual, separate from your baby who died. Then you can appreciate and accept your subsequent child for who he or she is, and not expect this child to be a replica of the baby who died.

> I had an amnio so I knew it was a girl, and I did that specifically for two reasons. One, I wanted to be able to say there are problems I know this baby won't have, and two, I wanted to know the sex because I had always wanted a girl and I knew that if it was a boy I was going to have that sense of loss to deal with and that if it was a girl I was going to have to work on separating her from Heidi. I remember when I got the results, being excited it was a girl but being really frustrated or sad and crying for a long time. The doctor said, "Well, you have a healthy baby girl." But I was thinking, "Why couldn't it have been Heidi."
>
> —Holly

> My neighbor was pregnant the same time I was and she had a boy about a month before I did and she brought

him in, and at first I thought, "This is really cruel." But I
held her baby and I realized, "This isn't my baby,
nobody's baby is going to take the place of my baby. This
isn't who I'm aching for. I'm aching for that specific baby,
MY baby." I was really relieved that she brought him
over and I didn't covet her baby.

—Bryn

Perhaps you would not have had your new baby if your other
baby hadn't died. Perhaps you feel as though you are trying to fill that
empty slot in your family. Whatever your intent, you will eventually
discover that this new baby can never totally erase your emptiness,
nor take your other baby's special place in your heart.

Some parents idealize the baby who died and impose those
perfect expectations on subsequent children. These parents inevita-
bly feel disappointment in the subsequent children, who cannot
possibly live up to the idealized image.

It can help to remember that all babies have fussy periods, need
a lot of attention and supervision, wake up during the night and go
through challenging stages. The reality of what's involved in parenting
can help you let go of your idealizations and be less resentful of your
surviving children. For instance, Bryn was able to finally let go of her
fantasies after her subsequent baby was born. She admits, "It helped
me to be exhausted in the middle of the night and saying, 'If she cries
one more time, how am I going to get up?' That helps to see the reality
of it, the good and the bad. It would have been so awful if I had not
been allowed to have a baby. It's so healthy to have reality there."

Most parents compare their babies without idealizing. The less
time you had with the baby who died, the more curious you may be.
It is natural to look at your subsequent children and wonder if the
baby who died would have been similar. Would they have had the
same curls? Would they have walked at the same age? Would they
have both resembled their father? Cindy remarks, "When you look
at Emily and see how she acts, you wonder if Nicole would have been
like her and looked like her and all that." Kitty agrees: "When Julie
was born she looked an awful lot like Melanie, so I kind of feel like
I can watch her grow up." It is natural to think about all the experiences you've missed with your baby, and to look at your subsequent
children and get an idea of what might have been. Liza observes: "It's

a feeling that you'd like to have five or six children so that all the personalities combined, you'd be able to see what the baby who died would be like."

Particularly if you have another baby of the same sex, it is natural to fear you will have trouble separating the two babies. It is natural to mix up their names, for instance, as most parents with more than one child do. Your dead baby is not living with you, but dwells in your heart, and his or her name may come to mind naturally.

> One time I slipped and I said "Nicole" instead of "Emily," and everybody went "GASP! Why did you do that? Are you going crazy? Are you confusing these babies? What's wrong with you?" And I cried and thought, "What's wrong?" And then my mom goes, "Would you people calm down? I mean, if she had two kids, one named Nicole, and Nicole was here and she said 'Nicole' to Emily or 'Emily' to Nicole, nobody would even give it thought, but because Nicole is dead everybody freaks out." She said, "We've talked about Nicole for a year. We go to her grave. Nicole is what we've called your baby all this time. We've talked about your baby Nicole, and now you slipped and said 'Nicole' instead of 'Emily': big deal!" But it scared me. I thought "Oh no, what's wrong with me?" And I've done it a couple times since then.
>
> —Cindy

This curiosity and comparison may not diminish over time because you will never know what that baby would have been like. However, as you get to know your new baby as an individual, rather than confusing the two babies, you may simply wonder how similar they might have been.

## POINTS TO REMEMBER

- Most parents feel that their relationship with surviving children, especially those born afterward, is profoundly affected by the death of their baby.
- It is normal to feel a greater appreciation for your surviving children.
- It is normal to feel overprotective, hoping to avoid another tragedy.
- Overprotective feelings diminish over time as you continue to work through your grief. These feelings may also fade as you become accustomed to having a child who can be healthy and survive and as your child grows more independent and competent.
- Harnessing your overprotective feelings can be difficult, but as you feel less vulnerable, letting go frees you from the burden of watching your child's every move.
- Avoid the unrealistic goal of being the perfect, selfless, cheerful parent in order to deserve this child you longed for. Instead, simply strive to do your best and learn from your mistakes.
- This enhanced sense of responsibility and devotion you feel can be aimed toward being a better, more nurturing parent. However, it is still normal to feel resentment and exhaustion at times.
- It is normal to worry about confusing your new baby with the baby who died.
- It is normal to look at your new baby and wonder if your dead baby might have been similar in appearance, personality or talent.
- It helps to have a realistic view of parenting, so that you do not idealize your baby who died and place those idealized expectations on your new baby.

# 12

# Remembering Your Baby And Moving On

You will always remember your baby. As you grieve and come to terms with your loss, you find that life goes on. Your sadness never completely disappears, but it does subside and acquire new meaning.

For many parents, grieving and surviving the death of a baby teaches them about life and about themselves. You may come through the experience with new coping skills, new friends and new insights. You may surprise yourself with the courage and stamina you have displayed. Liza observes, "I must be a lot stronger than I thought I was. I'm amazed that a person can reinvest in life after going through this."

You may feel more in touch with your feelings and understand the value of expressing them. You may be more sensitive to other bereaved people and better able to offer support. Meryl notes, "I think I found a lot more compassion for myself and for others—consideration, understanding, accepting other people *and* myself."

You may feel a heightened appreciation for the things you have; you may have straightened out your priorities. Holly remarks, "I value life more and my child more. I try not to take things for granted or dwell on picky little things that don't matter." Peg agrees: "It makes me aware of what's really important. I worry about the big things, try and deal with those, and I'm much calmer about the little things." Lena adds, "I treasure life more than I ever did—my own, my children's, even the ants on the driveway."

You may decide to give up trying to control those events that are out of your hands and put your energy into controlling those you can. Meryl comments, "It made me more accepting to life and that these things happen. Sometimes we have all the control in the world and other times, there isn't any control at all."

You may become more assertive. You may feel a sense of entitlement, that you deserve the best because you've been through the worst. You may be more able to stand up for yourself, to take care of yourself, to get what you need, instead of always sacrificing for others. Lena points out, "I have come to value more what I do and realizing I have to do things for me too. I can't be all things to all other people." Kelly agrees: "Now I look out for *me* first and then I do for others, because when he died I discovered nobody watches out for me, but me! Since I made this decision, I feel much better about myself and I have more self-respect." Rose elaborates, "I'm my own person now and I don't know if I'd have become that way if I hadn't lost Jessica. I think that forces you to get in touch with yourself, what you need."

You may also feel more self-reliant, that in a crisis you can count on yourself, but not necessarily others. You may feel wiser and older for your age, less naive, more vulnerable to life's twists and turns. Lena observes, "I've acquired the courage to face things I wouldn't have been able to face before as easily." Most parents eventually feel that through adversity, they have grown in some way that prepares them to cope with whatever the future holds.

> I had to come to grips with some pretty intense things
> about myself and I ended up liking myself and learning
> things about myself. I probably never would have learned
> had I not lost Jamie. People shouldn't have to learn those
> things that way, but I learned a lot of strengths that I had.
> Had someone told me my baby would die, I would've
> said, "Well, I just couldn't handle anything like that."
> Well, yes I could, I can, and I will again if I have to!
> —Sarah

# REMEMBERING

## *INTEGRATING YOUR BABY INTO THE FAMILY*

For many parents, a meaningful way to integrate the baby into the family is by telling their other children about the baby sibling who died. Particularly for your subsequent children, you may want them to know there was a brother or sister before them. To talk about the baby is another way to acknowledge his or her existence and to validate your love. Jessie comments, "I hold a place for her. She's still our first child and Lynn's older sister."

> Now I think of her more as a sister to my other children than I do the baby that I didn't have. We think of her as a part of our family, and Paul [age 6] talks about her. When Julie [age 1] is old enough to understand, she's going to understand that she did have a sister.
>
> —Kitty

> I know a lot of people who say, "Well, my mom had a stillborn," like that didn't really matter, it wasn't important. But that was your sister or brother! I want Emily to feel, "Yeah, I had a sister that was older than me, but she died and her name was Nicole."
>
> —Cindy

You may think that your subsequent children are too young to understand or appreciate the significance of a baby sibling who isn't around. Liza notes, "I've shown Michelle [age 3] his picture, but she just seems to think it's a little baby." You may decide to wait until your children are older or start asking questions. You may plan to share any mementos you have so they can get to know the baby.

> I want to wait until the kids are 8 or 9. I guess I want them to *understand*. I think they'll be sad and I think they'll want to go see the grave, but I don't want Meg going to kindergarten and bragging, "I had a brother" and showing off about it and chatting about it like it meant nothing. So I thought if she was a little older she might understand it. I just don't want it to become trite.
>
> —Bess

If you don't want to wait, you can try telling your children by explaining what happened and showing pictures and other mementos, but it may be a while before they can grasp the concept of death or of a sibling who isn't visible. If your children misinterpret what you tell them, you needn't be alarmed. Your children are simply fitting the information into their own intellectual framework. As they get older and more sophisticated, you can help them reorganize their ideas.

> I have a picture of him on my refrigerator, so when I look
> at him I say, "There's Matthew," and I take Alex [age 1]
> and I say, "That was your brother." He's too young to
> understand yet, but that's just how I am. And I say things
> like, "He would've liked you; you would've liked him."
>
> —Kara

> At one time Gary [age 3] wanted to know if he could dig
> Jamie up and play with him. I thought I did a really great
> job of explaining death to him, and then he asks, "Can
> we go dig him up and play with him?" Then I showed
> him a picture of Jamie, and you think you're so smart
> with your kids and you're just not. I thought I did this
> great discussion, "This is your brother, he died, etc.," and
> like a week later there's a picture of him at my mother's
> house—of him when he was a baby—and he said, "Oh
> look, there's me when I was dead." So I don't know what
> he understands.
>
> —Sarah

*WHEN PEOPLE ASK, "HOW MANY KIDS DO YOU HAVE?"*
Another way parents integrate the baby who died into the family is
to explain about all their children. You may decide to do this with
everyone or just certain people. Holly explains, "It depends on who
it is and how much of an explanation you want to get into and
whether you want to see their jaws fall open and have them feel like
they stuck their foot in their mouth." Hannah adds, "I sort of play it
by ear. If I don't say that I had her, I feel bad about it. But then I think,
'Well, I didn't want to get into a lengthy discussion, so it's OK.' "
Maya feels comfortable with this simple statement: "I have three
children; two are with me, and one died." Sherokee Ilse uses an even
simpler version: "I have two living children."

Even if you tell people, they may not recognize your baby as a
member of your family. Jessie points out, "It upsets me sometimes
when they see my 1-year-old and they say, 'Oh, this is your first child'
or 'This is your first Mother's Day.' I feel bad that Meghan is being
deprived of those things that were rightfully hers."

# MOVING ON

If you decide to have another baby or to adopt a child, being a parent can help you overcome feelings of failure or give you a window into what might have been. Parenthood can also add a sense of fullness to your life. Lena notices, "I feel like a much more caring, loving, nurturing person since having Ryan." Peg adds, "It kind of makes up for what I've been through. I don't feel like I'm waiting for something anymore." For many mothers, having a child to raise helps them to move on *and* remember, because this child is another link, a sibling to the baby who died.

> With Leslie being born, it really helped me because here
> was somebody who needed me. I wasn't going to be able
> to sit around and be depressed because I needed to be
> there for her. She helped me. She filled my life, she filled
> my hours. When she was 2 years old, somehow I could
> tell I was better.
>
> —Bryn

Whether you have a child to raise or not, it helps to realize that you are more things in this life than a parent. You are yourself first. You can live a full life, finding satisfaction in a wide variety of activities and interests. You can take on many roles among your relationships and work.

# REMEMBERING, MOVING ON

Memories are a way to hold on to what we've loved and lost. Although you move on, you take your memories with you. The memories do fade, but you will never totally forget them. Though your loss becomes less central to your life, you will keep a place in your heart for your baby who died.

> I really feel it's important you just don't forget about
> them. Christopher is a real part of our lives. And I'll never
> forget him. I don't want to.
>
> —Rayleen

After three years I finally could be who I am without being a person who had a dead baby. I finally separated myself from that ... but I can still picture him when I was holding him. Now I can't remember what his face looked like, but I can remember feeling the weight on my arm.

—Bryn

Instead of being on your mind all the time, it becomes part of your history. You know, you don't meet new people and discuss your dead baby anymore. I actually know people that don't know that I've lost a baby, and it isn't because I'm hiding it, it's just because it isn't part of my conversation. It just happened to me and I'll always be sad and I'll always have one less child.

—Sarah

# SONG FOR AN EMPTY CRADLE

*FOR ANDREA*

Out my bedroom window rests my gaze
Through the mist of emptiness and pain's grey haze
I watch the patterns softly formed and changed,
The hillsides' grasses gently rearranged
By the winds' caressing touch.

From my womb she fell; my breath was stilled
By fear and pain and yet my heart was filled
By the overwhelming wonder of what was Andrea
That now lay white and quiet in my hand.
My baby, my prayers, the life that I had planned

Were gone. And in their place was left
A desert. Hot and empty so bereft
of hope, save for the splintered dreams I'd planned
That shined like broken bottles in the sand.

And soon the minutes into long months turn,
And even with time's comfort still I yearn
To hold her once in warm embrace
And say goodbye, and yet, there is a place
I carry her still, within my heart, steadfast;
For even the briefest of memories last.

Out my bedroom window rests my gaze
Through the mist of emptiness and pain's grey haze.
I watch the patterns softly rearranged
And know my life, my dreams have all been changed.
My daughter's life was brief yet such
That in my emptiness I have so much.

—Clara Wilbrandt-Koenig

# A Note to Caregivers*

Whether you are a healthcare provider or a concerned friend or relative, you can offer invaluable support to bereaved parents. Here are some guidelines to keep in mind.

### FACE YOUR OWN FEELINGS ABOUT DEATH

Feelings of disappointment, failure, fear, sadness and anger over the death of a baby are quite natural. By acknowledging your own feelings, you will be better able to approach parents openly and supportively. They appreciate those who share their feelings and are comforted by knowing others grieve with them.

### EDUCATE YOURSELF ABOUT GRIEF

If you understand the impact of a baby's death on a family, you will be in a better position to offer support. Your awareness of the behavior and emotions that accompany grieving will enable you to reassure parents and help them realize their reactions are normal. You will also feel more comfortable around grieving parents.

### AFFIRM THE BABY

Personalize the parents' loss by referring to "the baby" and using the given name. Avoid using terms such as "products of conception" or "the stillbirth." Refrain from statements that devalue the baby who died, such as, "You're still young, you can have another." The

---

*Adapted from the author's article, "Perinatal Loss: Providing Support for Bereaved Parents," published in *Birth* 15:4, December 1988, pp. 242–246, by Blackwell Scientific Publications.

parents loved *this* baby. Don't try to persuade them to forget and move on—parents need to remember and dwell on the baby. By talking about the baby directly and sensitively, you can help parents acknowledge the loss and express their feelings. For those experiencing parenthood for the first time, however briefly, the idea that they are parents should be recognized.

### VALIDATE THE PARENTS' GRIEF

While the urge to ease parents' sorrow is natural, remember, there is nothing you can say or do that will take away their pain. Since the baby is constantly on their minds, avoiding the subject only makes them feel more isolated and invalidated. Refrain from statements that belittle their grief such as, "It's really for the best." They can only find silver linings for themselves at their own pace, and even then, these will not banish their grief. Instead of offering solutions or platitudes, simply tell them how sorry you are and that you are thinking of them. Knowing that you care and understand makes a difference.

### BE A WILLING LISTENER

Parents benefit from telling their story over and over. Even if you know the details, you might ask, "Would it help to tell me about your baby?" This is an invitation parents usually welcome. By listening with empathy and acceptance, you give the parent a chance to air thoughts and feelings without fear of judgment or pressure to "feel better by now." If the parent starts to cry, this is OK. They are crying healthy tears and you have given them an opportunity to express themselves.

### CONTINUE TO OFFER SUPPORT AS TIME PASSES

While the first year or so is most difficult, many parents feel abandoned or pressured to feel better after just a few weeks or months. Not wanting to burden you with their troubles, they may hesitate to discuss the baby or their feelings. If you pose general questions such as "How are you doing?" parents easily assume you only want to exchange pleasantries. Emotionally vulnerable, they may find it hard to seek out your support and choose to withdraw instead.

You can let them know you are thinking of them and the baby by broaching the subject. They will appreciate your initiative. You can demonstrate a willingness to listen by continuing to ask specific questions about their situation. Parents usually are eager to discuss matters such as: "What was the most difficult part about your baby's death?" or "What are some of your favorite memories?" or "What are some helpful and/or not so helpful things people have said to you?" Ask to see photographs or other mementos. If you have the opportunity, express your remembrance on the anniversary of the baby's due date, birth or death, or on special holidays. By inviting parents to share their grief, you will be providing genuine personal support.

If you work with bereaved parents in a clinical setting, consider these guidelines.

## GIVE CLEAR MEDICAL INFORMATION AND OPTIONS

Parents need factual, straightforward information on the medical condition of the baby and mother. Withholding information only builds resentment. Parents also benefit from making their own decisions, even the most difficult ones. It gives them a sense of control at a time when they are likely to feel powerless. Outline their options and factors to consider. Respect their decisions. Gather information about baptism, autopsy, disposal of the body and funeral arrangements so they will have access to it and time to consider what they want to do. Giving parents extra time allows them to overcome some of the shock as well as consider their options. The time factor is especially important for decisions that may be irreversible.

## EDUCATE THE PARENTS ABOUT GRIEF

Providing information can serve to encourage expression of emotions and reduce feelings of isolation. Prepare parents for the unexpected emotions and reactions that may occur: insomnia, fatigue, despair, anger and even illusions of seeing or hearing the baby—all are experienced by many other parents. When they feel discouraged, reassure them. Grieving takes time. Couples often benefit from reminders about the importance of communicating with each other and accepting their own grieving styles. If the opportunity exists, it is also helpful to educate their friends and relatives about what to expect and offer guidance as to how to be supportive.

## ENCOURAGE COLLECTING
## MEMORIES AND MEMENTOS

Medical staff are in a unique position to influence what can become vivid memories. If the situation is applicable, encourage parents to hold their dying baby. It may seem dramatic, but it gives them a special opportunity to nurture and comfort their child. Equally important, after death, offer them the chance to see and hold their baby—regardless of the age or developmental stage. Offering this opportunity more than once gives parents a chance to say their goodbyes. Parents need to spend ample time with the baby, particularly after medication and the initial shock have worn off. Save locks of hair, foot and hand prints, records of weight and length, hospital identification bracelets and clothing that the baby wore. Offer photographs of the baby or encourage parents to take their own.

## SHOW SENSITIVITY

Bereaved parents should be offered the choice of having a private room away from the maternity ward. Unlimited visiting allows the opportunity for additional support from family members and friends. Flagging the chart or door can help prevent staff from making inappropriate remarks about breast-feeding or infant care.

## BE AVAILABLE TO LISTEN

Let parents know you are available upon request. In their vulnerable state they may hesitate to ask for you—parents often feel unworthy of attention or do not want to impose. So, visit regularly and ask specific questions about their feelings and experience. Even if they are not responsive, they can benefit from your caring presence and your touch.

Listening can be difficult. Parents may direct their anger and feeling of helplessness toward medical staff members. They may blame you for the death of their baby. Don't take such outbursts personally. Instead, acknowledge their anger and empathize. This usually diffuses hostility. Remember that, in the long run, this kind of rage is healthier than self-blame, which can lead to self-destructive behavior and chronic depression.

## LIMIT SEDATIVE USE

While an occasional sedative can be useful for getting much needed sleep, they should not be routinely prescribed since they tend to dull the grief response. Parents who hide in a fog of sedatives will have more trouble working through their grief than those who can experience the intensity of their emotions. It is especially important for parents to be alert when making decisions or spending time with their baby.

## MAKE FOLLOW-UP CONTACTS AND REFERRALS

Parents need reassurance that their thoughts and feelings are reasonable and that they aren't losing their minds. Follow-up contacts by medical staff or parent groups can be helpful in reminding parents that shock, denial and overwhelming despair are necessary, but temporary, parts of the grieving process.

Many parents find counseling helpful, either as individuals or as a couple. Some parents are relieved that someone recognizes their need for counseling. Others may be in such a state of shock or denial that they do not respond to your support. In this case, a referral to a mental health professional can ensure they receive proper follow-up care. Make sure you refer parents to those counselors who understand the significance of the death of a baby.

## PROVIDE INFORMATION ABOUT
## ADDITIONAL RESOURCES

Offer or recommend books, articles or pamphlets that discuss causes, feelings and experiences surrounding pregnancy loss or infant death. These can provide parents with extra reassurance that their grief is normal and shared by others. Written materials also allow parents to absorb information at their own pace and to read over and over the passages that offer special comfort.

Pregnancy and infant loss support groups can be another valuable source of comfort. Sharing stories with other bereaved parents can validate feelings, reduce isolation and improve a couple's communication. Attending a support group can also offer hope for the future as parents observe how others have learned to cope. (See appendix B, "Resources for Bereaved Parents.")

## ORGANIZE STAFF SUPPORT

Encountering death can be disheartening, particularly for those dedicated to delivering healthy babies. You may find it difficult to handle the variety of parents' needs or be sensitive to every parent's individual preferences. Having regular perinatal mortality rounds is one way for staff to gather ideas and insight into supporting parents. By talking openly, you can also understand and alleviate some of the stress of dealing with death and grief. Finally, some healthcare providers can work with bereaved parents more easily than others, and they should be considered important resources.

# Resources for Bereaved Parents

*PUBLISHERS*
Call or write for information or catalogs.

Boulder County Hospice, Inc.
2825 Marine Street, Boulder, CO 80303
(303) 449-7740
    Sells *Death of a Dream* by Donna and Rodger Ewy.

Centering Corporation
Box 3367, Omaha, NE 68103-3367
(402) 553-1200
    Besides its own publications, Centering provides a nonprofit network for distributing supportive grief literature from other sources. From its comprehensive catalog you can order many of the books and pamphlets offered by the publishers listed here and the national support organizations listed below.

Creative Marketing
Human Services Division
2631 North Grand Avenue, East, Springfield, IL 62702
(217) 528-1756

National Maternal and Child Health Clearinghouse
38th and R Streets, N.W., Washington, DC 20057
(202) 625-8410
    Offers free, single copies of *A Guide to Resources in Perinatal Bereavement*, published in 1989 by the National Center for Education in Maternal and Child Health. The guide is a selected and annotated

list of resources, including books, booklets, pamphlets, brochures, professional journal articles, magazine articles, audiovisuals and organizations providing information and support to bereaved parents.

Perinatal Loss
2116 N.E. 18th Avenue, Portland, OR 97212
(503) 284-7426

Prairie Lark Press
Box 699-W, Springfield, IL 62705
(217) 544-6464, ext. 5275

Wintergreen Press
3630 Eileen Street, Maple Plain, MN 55359
(612) 476-1303

## NATIONAL ORGANIZATIONS

The Compassionate Friends, Inc.
National Office, Box 3696, Oak Brook, IL 60522-3696
(312) 990-0010
    A national, nondenominational self-help organization that offers support to bereaved parents and siblings, as well as brochures on coping with the death of a baby.

National SIDS Clearinghouse
8201 Greensboro Drive, Suite 600, McLean, VA 22102
(703) 821-8955
    Offers a variety of publications on SIDS.

National SIDS Foundation
2 Metro Plaza, Suite 205
8240 Professional Place, Landover, MD 20785
(800) 211-SIDS, in Maryland (301) 459-3388
    Provides information, counseling and referrals to families whose baby has died of SIDS, as well as community education, literature and films about SIDS, research, grief, infant death and apnea.

Pregnancy and Infant Loss Center
1415 East Wayzata Boulevard, Wayzata, MN 55391
(612) 473-9372

PILC is a nonprofit organization that offers families, friends and professional care providers information on education, counseling services and local, national and international support groups. PILC also publishes a newsletter, coordinates a parent-to-parent outreach program, distributes its own literature and materials produced by other organizations and provides professional training.

RESOLVE, Inc.
Box 474, Belmont, MA 02178
(617) 484-2424

Provides support and information about infertility.

Resolve Through Sharing
LaCrosse-Lutheran Hospital
1910 South Avenue, LaCrosse, WI 54601
(608) 785-0530, ext. 3675

Provides information on local and national parent support groups; training for professionals on counseling and follow-up of families who have experienced miscarriage, stillbirth or newborn death and offers literature for parents, healthcare providers and clergy.

SHARE (A Source of Help in Airing and Resolving Experiences)
Sister Jane Marie Lamb, Saint Elizabeth's Hospital
211 South Third Street, Belleville, IL 62222
(618) 234-2415

SHARE is a national nondenominational parent support organization that offers parents a place to express their feelings after the death of their baby. Offerings include a bimonthly newsletter written by parents and professionals, and information on nationwide and international meetings of SHARE and other parent support groups.

## FINDING A LOCAL SUPPORT GROUP

Call one of the national organizations listed above, your state self-help clearinghouse or contact the National Self-Help Clearinghouse.

National Self-Help Clearinghouse
33 West 42nd Street, New York, NY 10036
(212) 642-1944
    Provides information on pregnancy or infant loss support groups
for bereaved parents.

## FINDING A COUNSELOR
These national organizations may be able to give you information
about counselors or therapists in your area who have training in
helping bereaved parents.

American Psychiatric Association
1700 18th Street, N.W., Washington, DC 20009
(202) 797-4900

American Psychological Association
1200 17th Street, N.W., Washington, DC 20036
(202) 833-7600

Family Service Association of America
44 East 23rd Street, New York, NY 10010
(212) 674-6100

National Association of Social Workers
Supervisor of Registers and Directories
7981 Eastern Avenue, Silver Spring, MD 20910
(301) 565-0333

## HOSPICES
Hospices often have support services for the bereaved in their
community. These organizations can give you the names of hospices
in your area.

Children's Hospice International
Department P; Suite 131
1101 King Street, Alexandria, VA 22314

National Hospice Organization
1901 North Fort Myer Drive, Suite 307, Arlington, VA 22209
(703) 243-5900

# Bibliography

## PERIODICAL LITERATURE

Beck, M., et al. "Miscarriages." *Newsweek (August 15, 1988): 46–52* .

Benfield, D. G.; Leib, S. A.; and Vollman, J. H. "Grief Response of Parents to Neonatal Death and Parent Participation in Deciding Care." *Pediatrics* 62 (no. 2) (1978): 171–77.

Cain, A., and Cain, B. "On Replacing a Child." *American Academy of Child Psychiatry* 3 (1964): 443–55.

Carr, D., and Knupp, S. F. "Grief and Perinatal Loss: A Community Approach to Support." *Journal of Obstetric, Gynecologic, and Neonatal Nursing* 14 (1985): 130–39.

Chance, G. W., et al. "Support for Parents Experiencing Perinatal Loss." *Canadian Medical Association Journal* 129 (no. 4) (1983): 335–39.

Cohen, L., et al. "Perinatal Mortality: Assisting Parental Affirmation." *American Journal of Orthopsychiatry* 48 (no. 4) (1978): 727–31.

Condon, J. T. "Management of Established Pathological Grief Reaction after Stillbirth." *American Journal of Psychiatry* 143 (1986): 987–92.

———. "Prevention of Emotional Disability following Stillbirth—The Role of the Obstetric Team." *Australian and New Zealand Journal of Obstetrics and Gynecology* 27 (no. 4) (1987): 323–29.

Davidson, G. W. "Death of the Wished-for Child: A Case Study." *Death Education* 1 (1977): 265–75.

Davis, D. L. "Perinatal Loss: The Mother's Experience with Grief, Resolution and Subsequent Child." Ph.D. diss., Department of Psychology, University of Massachusetts, Amherst, 1986.

Davis, D. L.; Stewart, M; and Harmon, R. J. "Perinatal Loss: Providing Emotional Support for Bereaved Parents." *Birth* 15 (no. 4) (1988):242–46.

———. "Postponing Pregnancy after Perinatal Death: Perspectives on Doctors' Advice." *Journal of the American Academy of Child and Adolescent Psychiatry* 28 (no. 3) (1989): 481–87.

Davis, J. A. "Management of Perinatal Loss of a Twin." *British Medical Journal* 297 (no. 6663) (1988): 1613.

Dyregrov, A., and Matthiesen, S. B. "Anxiety and Vulnerability in Parents Following the Death of an Infant." *Scandinavian Journal of Psychology* 28 (no. 1) (1987): 16–25.

———. "Similarities and Differences in Mothers' and Fathers' Grief Following the Death of an Infant." *Scandinavian Journal of Psychology* 28 (no. 1) (1987): 1–15.

Elliot, B. A. "Neonatal Death: Reflections for Parents."*Pediatrics* 62 (no. 1) (1978): 100–102.

Elliot, B. A., and Hein, H. A. "Neonatal Death: Reflections for Physicians." *Pediatrics* 62 (no. 1) (1978): 96–99.

Furlong, R. M., and Hobbins, J. C. "Grief in the Perinatal Period." *Obstetrics and Gynecology* 61 (no. 4) (1983): 497–500.

Harmon, R. J.; Glicken, A. D.; and Siegel, R. E. "Neonatal Loss in the Intensive Care Nursery: Effects on Maternal Grieving and a Program for Intervention." *Journal of the American Academy of Child Psychiatry* 23 (1984): 68–71.

Helmrath, T. A., and Steinitz, E. M. "Death of an Infant: Parental Grieving and the Failure of Social Support." *The Journal of Family Practice* 6 (no. 4) (1978): 785–90.

Hildebrand, W. L., and Schreiner, R. L. "Helping Parents Cope with Perinatal Death." *American Family Physician* 22 (no. 5), (1980):121–25.

Johnson, J. "Guiding Children through Grief." *Mothering* (51) (1989): 29–35.

———. "When Things Go Wrong: What to Do if Your Newborn Dies."*Mothering* (39) (1986): 26–29.

Kirkley-Best, E., and Kellner, K. R. "The Forgotten Grief: A Review of the Psychology of Stillbirth."*American Journal of Orthopsychiatry* 52 (1982): 420–29.

Kirkley-Best, E.; Kellner, K. R.; and Ladue, T. "Attitudes Toward Stillbirth and Death Threat Level in a Sample of Obstetricians."*Omega: Journal of Death and Dying* 15 (1984): 317–27.

Kirkley-Best, E., and VanDevere, C. "The Hidden Family Grief: An Overview of Grief in the Family Following Perinatal Death." *International Journal of Family Psychiatry* 7 (no. 4) (1986): 419–37.

Kowalski, K. "Perinatal Death: An Ethnomethodological Study of Factors Influencing Parental Bereavement." Ph.D. diss., Department of Sociology, University of Colorado, Boulder, 1984.

LaFerla, J. J.,and Good, R. S. "Helping Patients Cope with Pregnancy Loss." *Contemporary OB/GYN* 25 (no. 4) (1985): 106–15.

LaRoche, C., et al. "Grief Reactions to Perinatal Death: A Follow-up Study." *Canadian Journal of Psychiatry* 29 (1984):14–19.

Leon, I. G. "Psychodynamics of Perinatal Loss." *Psychiatry* 49 (1986): 312–24.

Leppert, P. C., and Pahlka, B. S. "Grieving Characteristics after Spontaneous Abortion: A Management Approach." *Obstetrics and Gynecology* 64 (no. 1) (1984): 119–22.

Lewis, E., and Page, A. "Failure to Mourn a Stillbirth: An Overlooked Catastrophe." *British Journal of Medical Psychology* 51 (1978): 237–41.

Lindemann, E. "Symptomatology and Management of Acute Grief." *American Journal of Psychiatry* 101 (no. 2) (1944): 141–48.

Mandell, F.; McClain, M.; and Reece, R. "The Sudden Infant Death Syndrome: Siblings and Their Place in the Family." *Annals of the New York Academy of Sciences* 533 (1988): 129–31.

Martocchio, B. C. "Grief and Bereavement: Healing through Hurt." *Nursing Clinics of North America* 20 (no. 2) (1985): 327–41.

Murray, J., and Callan, V. J. "Predicting Adjustment to Perinatal Death." *British Journal of Medical Psychology* 61 (no. 3)(1988): 237–44.

Nichol, M. T., et al. "Maternal Grieving Response after Perinatal Death." *Medical Journal of Australia* 144 (1986): 287–89.

Parkes, C. M. "The First Year of Bereavement." *Psychiatry* 33 (1970): 444–67.

Peppers, L. G., and Knapp, R. J. "Maternal Reactions to Involuntary Fetal/Infant Death." *Psychiatry* 43 (1980): 155–59.

Phipps, S. "The Subsequent Pregnancy after Stillbirth: Anticipatory Parenthood in the Face of Uncertainty." *International Journal of Psychiatry and Medicine* 15 (1985): 243–64.

Poznanski, E. O. "The Replacement Child: A Saga of Unresolved Parental Grief." *Behavioral Pediatrics* 81 (no. 6) (1972): 1190–93.

Queenan, J. "Never Underestimate the Help You Can Offer Bereaved Parents." *Contemporary Obstetrics and Gynecology* 12 (1978): 9–10.

Rosenblatt, P. G., and Burns, L. H. "Long-term Effects of Perinatal Loss." *Journal of Family Issues* 7 (no. 3) (1986): 237–53.

Rowe, J., et al. "Follow–up of Families Who Experience Perinatal Death." *Pediatrics* 62 (no. 2) (1978): 166–70.

Rubin, S. S. "Mourning Distinct from Melancholia: The Resolution of Bereavement." *British Journal of Medical Psychology* 57 (1984):339–45.

Saylor, D. E. "Nursing Response to Mothers of Stillborn Infants." *Journal of Obstetrical and Gynecological Nursing* 6 (no. 4) (1977): 39–42.

Sculpholme, A. "Coping with the Unexpected Outcomes of Pregnancy." *Journal of Obstetrical and Gynecological Nursing* 7 (no. 3) (1978): 36–39.

Seitz, P. M., and Warrick, L. H. "Perinatal Death: The Grieving Mother." *American Journal of Nursing* 74 (no. 11) (1974): 2028–33.

Speck, W. T., and Kennell, J. H. "Management of Perinatal Death." *Pediatrics in Review* 2 (1980): 59–62.

Sperhac, A. M. "Sudden Infant Death Syndrome." *Nurse Practitioner* 7 (no. 8) (1982): 3844.

Stack, J. M. "The Psychodynamics of Spontaneous Abortion." *The American Journal of Orthopsychiatry* 54 (no. 1) (1984): 16267.

———. "Spontaneous Abortion and Grieving." *American Family Physician* 21 (no. 5) (1980): 99–102.

Stierman, E. D. "Emotional Aspects of Perinatal Death." *Clinical Obstetrics and Gynecology* 30 (no. 2) (1987): 352–61.

Stringham, J. G.; Riley, J. H.; and Ross, A. "Silent Birth: Mourning a Stillborn Baby." *Social Work* 27 (no. 4) (1982): 322–27.

Theut, S. K., et al. "Perinatal Loss and Parental Bereavement." *American Journal of Psychiatry* 146 (no. 5) (1989): 635–39.

Theut, S. K., et al. "Pregnancy Subsequent to Perinatal Loss: Parental Anxiety and Depression." *Journal of the American Academy of Child and Adolescent Psychiatry* 27 (1988): 289–92.

Tomsyck, R. R. "The Grief of a Mother/Physician on the Death of Her Infant." *Journal of the American Medical Women's Association* 43 (no. 2) (1988): 51–57.

Tudehope, D. I., et al. "Neonatal Death: Grieving Families." *Medical Journal of Australia* 144 (1986): 290–92.

Videka-Sherman, L., and Lieberman, M. "The Effects of Self-help and Psychotherapy Intervention on Child Loss: The Limits of Recovery." *American Journal of Orthopsychiatry* 55 (no. 1) (1985): 70–82.

Wasserman, A. L. "Helping Families Get through the Holidays after the Death of a Child." *American Journal of Diseases of Children* 142 (no. 12) (1988): 1284–86.

Wilson, A. L., et al. "The Death of a Newborn Twin: An Analysis of Parental Bereavement." *Pediatrics* 70 (1982): 587–591.

Wilson, A. L., et al. "Parental Response to Perinatal Death: Mother-Father Differences." *American Journal of Diseases of Children* 139 (no. 12) (1986): 1235–38.

Wilson, A. L., and Soule, D. J. "The Role of a Self-help Group in Working with Parents of a Stillborn Baby." *Death Education* 5 (1981): 175–86.

Woodward, S., et al. "Bereavement Counseling after Sudden Infant Death." *British Medical Journal* 290 (1985): 363–65.

Wortman, C. B., and Silver, R. C. "The Myths of Coping with Loss." *Journal of Consulting and Clinical Psychology* 57 (no. 3) (1989): 349–57.

Zahourek, R., and Jensen, J. S. "Grieving and the Loss of a Newborn." *American Journal of Nursing* 73 (no. 5) (1973): 836–39.

Zeanah, C. H. "Adaptation following Perinatal Loss: A Critical Review." *Journal of the American Academy of Child and Adolescent Psychiatry* 28 (no. 3) (1988): 467–80.

## BOOKS FOR HEALTHCARE PROVIDERS

Arnold, J. H., and Gemma, P. B. *A Child Dies: A Family Portrait*. Rockville, Md.: Aspen Systems Corporation, 1983.

Bowlby, J. *Attachment and Loss*. Vol. 3, *Loss*. New York: Basic Books, 1980.

Edelstein, L. *Maternal Bereavement: Coping with the Unexpected Death of a Child*. New York: Praeger, 1984.

Hollingsworth, C. E., and Pasnau, R. O., eds. *The Family in Mourning: A Guide for Health Professionals*. New York: Grune and Stratton, 1977.

Jackson, E. N. *Understanding Grief*. Nashville, Tenn.: Abingdon Press, 1957.

Jonsen, A. R., and Garland, M. J., eds. *Ethics of Newborn Intensive Care.* The Regents of the University of California: Health Policy Program and Institute of Governmental Studies, 1976.

Kennell, M. H., and Klaus, J. H. "Caring for Parents of a Stillborn or an Infant Who Dies." In *Maternal-Infant Bonding,* edited by J. H. Klaus and M. H. Kennell. Saint Louis: The C. V. Mosby Company, 1982.

Leon, I. G. *When a Baby Dies: Psychotherapy for Pregnancy and Newborn Loss.* New Haven, Conn.: Yale University Press, 1990.

Limbo, R. K., and Wheeler, S. R. *When a Baby Dies: A Handbook for Healing and Helping.* LaCrosse, Wisc.: Resolve Through Sharing, 1986.

Parkes, C. M. *Bereavement: Studies of Grief in Adult Life.* New York: International Universities Press, Inc., 1972.

Parkes, C. M., and Weiss, R. S. *Recovery from Bereavement.* New York: Basic Books, Inc., Publishers, 1983.

Peppers, L. G., and Knapp, R. *Motherhood and Mourning: Perinatal Death.* New York: Praeger, 1980.

Rando, T. A., ed. *Parental Loss of a Child.* Champaign, Ill.: Research Press, 1986.

Woods, J. R., and Esposito, J. L., eds. *Pregnancy Loss: Medical Therapeutics and Practical Considerations.* Baltimore: Williams and Wilkins, 1987.

## BOOKS FOR BEREAVED PARENTS

Berezin, N. *After a Loss in Pregnancy: Help for Families Affected by Miscarriage, a Stillbirth, or the Loss of a Newborn.* New York: Simon and Schuster, 1982.

Borg, S., and Lasker, J. *When Pregnancy Fails: Families Coping with Miscarriage, Ectopic Pregnancy, Stillbirth and Infant Death.* Rev. ed. New York: Bantam Books, 1988.

DeFrain, J., et al. *Stillborn—The Invisible Death.* Lexington, Mass.: D.C. Heath/Lexington Books, 1986.

DeFrain, J.; Taylor, J.; and Ernst, L. *Coping with Sudden Infant Death.* Lexington, Mass.: D.C. Heath/Lexington Books, 1982.

Ewy, D., and Ewy, R. *Death of a Dream.* New York: E. P. Dutton, Inc., 1984. Out of print, but available through Boulder County Hospice: see appendix B, "Resources for Bereaved Parents."

Friedman, R., and Gradstein, B. *Surviving Pregnancy Loss.* Boston: Little, Brown and Company, 1982.

Ilse, S. *Empty Arms: Coping with Miscarriage, Stillbirth and Infant Death.* Maple Plain, Minn.: Wintergreen Press, 1990.

Ilse, S., and Burns, L. H. *Miscarriage: A Shattered Dream.* Maple Plain, Minn.: Wintergreen Press, 1985.

Jackson, E. N. *You and Your Grief.* New York: Hawthorn Books, Inc., 1962.

Jimenez, S. L. M. *The Other Side of Pregnancy: Coping with Miscarriage and Stillbirth.* Englewood Cliffs, N.J.: Prentice-Hall, Inc., 1982.

Kushner, H. S. *When Bad Things Happen to Good People.* Boston: Beacon Press, 1981.

Panuthos, C., and Romeo, C. *Ended Beginnings: Healing Childbearing Losses.* South Hadley, Mass.: Bergin and Garvey Publishers, Inc., 1984.

Peppers, L. G., and Knapp, R. *How to Go on Living after the Death of a Baby.* Atlanta: Peachtree Publishers, 1985.

Pizer, H., and Palinski, C. O. *Coping with Miscarriage.* New York: New American Library/Plume Books, 1980.

Rando, T. A. *Grieving: How to Go on Living When Someone You Love Dies.* Lexington, Mass.: D.C. Heath/Lexington Books, 1988.

Salzer, L. P. *Infertility: How Couples Can Cope.* Boston: G. K. Hall & Co., 1986.

Schiff, H. S. *The Bereaved Parent.* New York: Penguin, 1978.

## PERSONAL ACCOUNTS

Berg, B. *Nothing to Cry About.* New York: Harper and Row, 1981.

Fischhoff, J., and Brohl, N. O. *Before and After My Child Died: A Collection of Parents' Experiences.* Detroit: Emmons-Fairfield Publishing Co., 1981.

Fritsch, J., and Ilse, S. *The Anguish of Loss.* Maple Plain, Minn.: Wintergreen Press, 1988.

Galinsky, H. *Beginnings.* New York: Houghton Mifflin, 1976.

Hill, S. *Family.* New York: Viking, 1989.

Jensen, A. H. *Healing Grief.* Redmond, Wash.: Medic, 1980.

Kotzwinkle, W. *Swimmer in the Secret Sea.* New York: Avon, 1975.

Landorf, J., *Mourning Song.* Old Tappan, N.J.: Fleming H. Revell Co., 1974.

Massanari, J., and Massanari, A. *Our Life with Caleb.* Philadelphia: Fortress Press, 1976.

Putnam, C. H. "Losing Jacob." *The Sunday Camera Magazine* (Boulder, Colo.), November 19, 1989, 1–9.

Vredevelt, P. W. *Empty Arms: Emotional Support for Those Who Have Suffered Miscarriage or Stillbirth.* Portland, Ore.: Multnomah Press, 1984.

## BOOKS FOR PARENTS AND CHILDREN

Bernstein, J. E. *Loss and How to Cope with It.* New York: Seabury, 1977. (For older children and teens.)

Brown, M. W. *The Dead Bird.* Reading, Mass.: Addison-Wesley, 1965. (For young children.)

Carrick, C. *The Accident.* New York: Seabury, 1976. (For young children.)

Grollman, E. A., ed. *Explaining Death to Children.* Boston: Beacon Press, 1979. (For parents.)

Jewett, C. L. *Helping Children Cope with Separation and Loss.* Harvard, Mass.: The Harvard Common Press, 1982. (For parents.)

Kantrowitz, M. *When Violet Died.* New York: Parents' Magazine Press, 1973. (For young children.)

Kaplan, B. *The Empty Chair.* New York: Harper and Row, 1978. (For older children and teens.)

Rofes, E. E., and the Unit at Fayerweather Street School. *The Kid's Book about Death and Dying.* Boston: Little, Brown and Company, 1985. (For older children.)

Schaefer, D., and Lyon, C. *How Do We Tell the Children? A Parent's Guide to Helping Children Understand and Cope When Someone Dies.* New York: Newmarket Press, 1985. (For parents.)

Viorst, J. *The Tenth Good Thing About Barney.* New York: Atheneum, 1971. (For younger and older children.)

White, E. B. *Charlotte's Web.* New York: Harper, 1952. (For older children.)

Zim, H., and Bleeker, S. *Life and Death.* New York: Morrow, 1970. (For older children and teens.)

## BOOKS ON PARENTING

Boddie, C. F. *The Feelings Book: Expressing Emotions Creatively, A Guide for Children and Grownups.* Evergreen, Colo.: Cordillera Press, 1988.

Bradshaw, J. *Bradshaw On: The Family.* Deerfield Beach, Fla.: Health Communications, 1988.

Brown, J. R. *"I Only Want What's Best for You": A Parent's Guide to Raising Emotionally Healthy Children.* New York: St. Martin's Press, 1986.

Dinkmeyer, D., and McKay, G. D. *The Parent's Handbook: Systematic Training for Effective Parenting.* 3rd ed. Circle Pines, Minn.: American Guidance Service, 1989.

Dinkmeyer, D., McKay, G. D., and Dinkmeyer, J. S. *Parenting Young Children.* Circle Pines, Minn.: American Guidance Service, 1989.

Faber, A., and Mazlish, E. *How to Talk So Kids Will Listen and Listen So Kids Will Talk.* New York: Rawson, Wade Publishers, 1982.

———. *Siblings Without Rivalry: How to Help Your Children Live Together So You Can Live Too.* New York: Avon Books, 1987.

Gordon, T. *Parent Effectiveness Training.* New York: New American Library, 1975.

Greenspan, S., and Greenspan, N. T. *First Feelings: Milestones in the Emotional Development of Your Baby and Child.* New York: Viking Penguin, 1985.

Nelson, J. *Positive Discipline.* New York: Ballantine Books, 1987.

Salk, L. *Your Child's First Year.* New York: Simon and Schuster, 1983.

Sears, W. *The Fussy Baby: How to Bring out the Best in Your High-need Child.* New York: New American Library, 1985.

———. *Nighttime Parenting: How to Get Your Baby and Child to Sleep.* Franklin Park, Ill.: La Leche League International, 1985.

# Index